WHITE FUNNEL MEMORIES

Bristol Queen leaving Bristol, 1949. Captain Jack George on telegraphs and George Gunn, mate, at the wheel.

WHITE FUNNEL MEMORIES

George Gunn

GOMER

First Impression—May 1997

ISBN 1 85902 487 4

Printed at
Gomer Press, Llandysul, Ceredigion

Dedicated
to the Memory
of Fine Ships
and
Good Shipmates

CONTENTS

		page
Foreword		9
Preface		11
Introduction		13
First Impressions		17
White Funnel Captains		19
White Funnel Guv'nors		25
Chocolate Boy to Chief Steward		27
White Funnel Ships		29
	Ravenswood	29
	Bristol Queen	33
	Empress Queen	33
	Glen Usk	36
	Glen Gower	41
	Cardiff Queen	42
	Britannia	45
Sisterly Rivalry		49
White Funnel Pursers		52
White Funnel Engineers		54
Easter Sailings		56
White Funnel Places		58
Channel Characters		68
Shipboard Entertainment		71
Wintering with Campells		72
The Bristol Channel Hovercraft		76
A Bristol Channel Vehicle Ferry: costs and complications		78
Epilogue		80

FOREWORD

I was extremely pleased when I was asked by Captain George Gunn, author of *White Funnel Memories*, to provide this Foreword.

This book traces the post-War passenger steamers in the Bristol Channel from 1948 through to the 1970s. It contains many interesting photographs of the ships and the personnel involved in their operation. It is not meant to be technical, but rather to give some inside information on what went on during that period.

I have known George Gunn for many years, since we served together as elected members on the former Swansea City Council.

Having held office as the last Lord Mayor of that authority in 1995-6, it gives me great pleasure to be associated with this publication.

Grenville Phillips

Cardiff Queen passing King's Dock entrance at Swansea bound for Ilfracombe in June 1958. It was the author's last year in command of the ship. The Port activity can be seen in the background with all general cargo berths full. The war-ravaged approach jetty on the starboard side of the lock is out of use and under renewal. This facility was sorely missed when docking ships during tide time and when vessels were awaiting the first lock on the next tide.

(Photo: World Ship Society Collection)

PREFACE

DETAILED HISTORIES OF the lovely ships of the White Funnel Fleet, since the arrival of P.&A. Campbell's *Waverley* in the Bristol Channel in 1887, are well documented. This book is not an attempt to add to histories of that sort, but rather a reflection on my own experiences of the ships, and on the characters and the folklore of that most famous of excursion-steamer fleets.

Of my fifty years in the shipping industry, only twelve or so were spent on the bridges of Campbell ships, but It was a memorable, eventful and important part of my life. During that time I sailed with, and met, a wonderful cross-section of people, working and travelling on the ships.

Having been in charge of all post-War White Funnel paddle steamers at one time or another, I have been encouraged by members of the Paddle Steamer Preservation Society to put some memories of those happy times on paper. This book is the result.

I wish to make it clear that the views and opinions expressed here are mainly from my own recollections of people and events of the day. I hope they will provide some interesting information about the steamers, and those who 'kept the wheels turning'.

I am indebted to: Paul Elkin and Andy King of the Bristol Industrial Museum who facilitated publication of the book by accessing many hitherto unpublished photographs from the superb Keen collection held by the Museum; Hugh John, Swansea City Council photographer for his help and advice; Syd Gray, an old friend and shipmate for his personal contribution; Mrs Hopkins, for aerial photographs taken by her late husband, Victor; George Owen, White Funnel photographic historian.

My particular thanks go to Nick James for his close co-operation in the compilation of the book, and to many members of the Paddle Steamer Preservation Society who encouraged me to write it.

Captain George Gunn

The classic white-funnel paddle steamer *Glen Gower* leaving Bristol on a cruise, on 29 July 1951. Captain Gunn is clearly visible on the bridge-wing.

INTRODUCTION

Peter and Alex Campbell's decision to leave their home waters of the Clyde and transfer their long-established family steamer operations to the Bristol Channel in 1887 cannot have been an easy one to make. Operating paddle steamers in the comparatively sheltered waters of the Firth of Clyde was a very different enterprise to that experienced in the very strong tidal waters of the Channel, exposed to the full force of Atlantic westerlies and with few ports available, particularly at low water, when the weather turned nasty.

'The Old Guv'nor', Captain Peter Campell looking aft on *Ravenswood*. It was difficult to see ahead with the two funnels in front of him: he had *that* altered.

What drove Campbells from the Clyde was railway competition to the routes which they plied. In the Bristol Channel, although there was little competition from the railways, there was competition from other steamer operators. Peter and Alex Campbell thrived on fair competition. Having been brought up with excursion steamers, and with their own individual shipping experience and high marine qualifications, the Campbell brothers took on all others, and won. Their White Funnel Fleet had, by 1922, eliminated all opposition, and the influence and expertise of the Campbell brothers, and particularly of Captain Peter, still pervaded the Company. It continued to do so right through until the early 'fifties,when both brothers were long dead. So it was that I found myself under their influence, and Peter Campbell was still referred to as the 'old guv'nor'.

I have often been asked how I ever became master of a paddle steamer. It was quite easy—passing Hotwells Dock in Bristol as second mate of a cargo vessel in April 1948, I saw a colourful collection of small ships wedged in there preparing for summer service in the Channel. That was my first ever sighting of Campbell's steamers. A short walk from our berth at Canons Marsh to their offices at Cumberland Basin resulted in an appointment as first mate.

My first ship was the veteran *Ravenswood* of 1891, and the first purpose-built Bristol Channel Campbell paddler. She was lying at the pontoon at Cardiff when I joined her in June 1948, and being low water, she was aground on the mud. This was the first of many new experiences, but 'drying out' in the Bristol Channel ports of Newport, Cardiff and Swansea was soon to become a regular feature of this unique job. Putting ships aground on mud is fine when intended, yet frowned upon when not.

The first person I met aboard *Ravenswood* that day was her chief engineer, Alex Campbell, one of two sons of the founder of the company, and the last of the Campbell family to serve on board its ships. His opening remarks were that new mates usually started on

Ravenswood—she was the oldest and could be knocked about a bit without much showing. Alex was a rotund, easy-going character, some would say almost irresponsible, but he proved to be a good friend and shipmate throughout the time we sailed together. He had survived the sinking of the *Glen Avon* which had foundered at anchor off the Normandy coast in 1944 when the weather turned bad. It must be said that even during the War it was difficult for a person in charge of a ship to explain its loss under these circumstances. Every Merchant Navy officer with a ticket of any kind would have found little difficulty in releasing the anchor without endangering the ship. *Glen Avon*'s capstan may have failed at the wrong time, but Alex found a lifebuoy floating towards him at just the right time.

Ravenswood was aptly nicknamed 'The Scratcher'; as the tide rose, she was expected to get into places earlier than other ships, and, as it fell, scrape out later.

Campbells had enjoyed a bumper year in 1947 with a handsome operating profit of £99,000. Unfortunately my first season of 1948 was not such a successful one, with persistent strong winds and heavy rain. Luckily, 1949 came good again with weather and passenger numbers. I was then mate of the flagship *Bristol Queen* with the legendary Captain George. We sailed daily from Bristol to Clevedon, Cardiff, Penarth, Barry, Lynmouth and Ilfracombe, sometimes via Weston with connections from Cardiff or Newport. After Ilfracombe, we often headed further west for an afternoon cruise or further still to Lundy,

Glen Gower, Britannia, Cardiff Queen, Bristol Queen, off Ilfracombe, July 1950. The captains, respectively, were Joe Phillips, Archie Harris, Bert Murphy and Jack George.

then all the way back again to berth in Cumberland Basin overnight and prepare for the next day's run. Bristol to Lundy and back is 194 nautical miles—not bad for a day-excursion by paddle steamer. Lateness would mean missing the tide in the Avon, and was therefore strictly forbidden.

By 1948, all the vessels were deployed on what were considered their most suitable stations: *Bristol Queen* on the Bristol to Ilfracombe run, *Cardiff Queen* from Cardiff down-Channel, *Glen Usk*—the mainstay and the Company's breadwinner—the Cardiff to Weston ferry, with cruises from Barry and Clevedon at low-water times. *Ravenswood* was the Newport to Weston boat, and supplemented *Glen Usk* on the Cardiff to Weston ferry, which was the jewel in the crown of Bristol Channel operations until the Severn Bridge interfered in 1966. *Britannia*, *Glen Gower* and *Empress Queen* completed the fleet of White Funnel ships serving the Bristol and English Channels. *Glen Gower* was based at Swansea, the other two on the South Coast. *Empress Queen*—Campbell's only turbine screw steamer—had been built for no-passport trips to France, which were denied to her because of the extension of wartime regulations. She was quite unsuited to trying to make a living cruising along the English Channel coast and around the Isle of Wight.

When I joined Campbells, therefore, they were firmly back in business after the trauma of war. Twelve of their ships had gone to war; seven returned, of which two were scrapped as unfit for further service. The five survivors plus the two new paddlers *Bristol Queen* and *Cardiff Queen* made up the UK's finest fleet of passenger excursion steamers. P.& A. Campbell were very much back in business.

This was reflected in more ways than one. Every master and chief engineer appointed to the ships in 1948 was a pre-War experienced Bristol- and English-Channel man: Captain Shedden, *Ravenswood*; Joe Phillips, *Britannia*; Bert Murphy, *Glen Gower*; Findley Brander, *Glen Usk*; Jack George, *Bristol Queen*; Archie Harris, *Cardiff Queen*; Bill Couves, *Empress Queen*.

It was a different story with the mates. With the exception of Jimmy Martin and Bill Watson we were all new to the paddle boat scene, having spent the War years and afterwards on British merchant ships trading throughout the world, and now seeing this as a 'home job' at last.

Captain Jack George, in pensive mood.

15

Bert Murphy, moving ship in Cumberland Basin, Bristol.

The Campbell ships were also covered by a nucleus of pre-War pursers, senior stewards and bosuns. Campbell's men ashore and afloat sprouted from all over the place, back to their old jobs. For them, it was a return, at least until post-War realities became all too evident, to a world with which they were thoroughly familiar. For me, as a newcomer, it was the beginning of a unique experience, as I lived and worked through the beginning of the end of the Campbell empire.

FIRST IMPRESSIONS

Campbell's paddle steamers carried millions of passengers over a period of more than a hundred years without a single loss of life. This proud record was due in no small way to the specialist expertise of the officers and crews who manned the vessels. As a seasoned seaman and ships' officer when I joined the White Funnel Fleet, it was difficult for me to understand how this remarkable record was maintained. There are few areas of the world where weather and tidal conditions are as tough to contend with as in the Bristol Channel, so good luck must sometimes have gone hand-in-hand with experience and efficiency.

Navigation aids and manoeuvring facilities on all these ships 45 years ago were very basic. The bridge had a single magnetic steering compass; a teakwood box to keep your binoculars in and a notebook to record engine movements, courses and times. There were engine and docking telegraphs; communication voice pipes to the purser and engineer; a lanyard to blow the steam whistle; and nothing else.

None of the paddle steamers had a wheelhouse. The open bridge concept prevailed throughout the years, it being the opinion of older officers that a wheelhouse would be too restrictive for berthing at piers and pontoons and navigating rivers such as the Avon and the Usk. *Bristol Queen* was designed to take a wheelhouse, but they didn't want it. Protection against wind and rain was a two-foot canvas dodger around the fore end of the bridge. We had a perspex one made for *Cardiff Queen*, which was a slight advance. 'Weather-beaten' would be a fair description of the state of deck officers on Campbells steamers at the end of an operating season.

The open bridge concept meant that sou'westers, oilskins and seaboots were sometimes the rig of the day. This was occasionally supplemented by a P.&A.C. face towel around the neck to protect white collars, particularly paper ones, which disintegrated when exposed to steady, heavy rain. New boys were informed that in days gone by a poor view was taken of masters and mates bringing ships alongside piers

Ravenswood, 1948. Afternoon cruise from Barry

over-dressed for bad weather. The 'old guv'nor' felt it might make some apprehensive waiting passengers disinclined to travel. Although the 'old guv'nor' was no longer with us, the message was passed on, received and understood.

During the 1950s and 1960s an immense volume of shipping used Bristol-Channel ports. Cross-Channel services of the White Funnel Fleet cut almost at right angles to the busy lanes of traffic. Some of

Bristol Queen, 1954, captained by Jack George.

navigation equipment on the bridge, so in poor visibility and dodgy weather conditions, with up to 1,000 passengers on board, it was a responsible and apprehensive job. Ships' officers who had sailed for a number of years with radar sometimes forgot that many of the large moving targets they plotted on their screens didn't have it, and that they themselves could not be seen in fog.

Glen Gower was the first Campbell paddler to have a radar set fitted, inherited from the large turbine *Empress Queen*, and set up in a wooden box on the open bridge for protection against the elements. It was a requirement for her 'no passport' trips to France. Perhaps the following anecdote illustrates changing attitudes of the time. In the mid-1960s as a Swansea Harbour Pilot I went on board to sail a loaded Cardiff collier. The master said he had no third mate this trip. One had joined that afternoon, and said to him, 'I don't see any radar here, Captain, this ship's no good to me.' Captain Bishop responded, 'If that's the case, you're no good to me either.'

Captain George Gunn mooring at Ilfracombe.

(Photo: Nigel Coombes)

these vessels had radar, but many didn't, and that was a problem. The speed of ships since the War had increased considerably, and with a strong flood or ebb tide behind them, moved along at up to eighteen knots. Before the War similar types of ships had generally been several knots slower, and very few of them faster than Campbell's paddle steamers. Because of their deep drafts and what they considered limited manoeuvring space in the Channel, they had no intention of making any unnecessary alteration of course. The well-known saying at sea that 'coastal masters worried when they lost sight of land; deep sea masters worried when they saw it' (or colloquial words to that effect) was often the case in the confines of the Bristol Channel. The Rule of the Road wasn't always followed and often had to be ignored completely. The interests of safety and survival were best served by giving way and altering course in plenty of time.

None of Campbell's steamers had radar, or any other modern

WHITE FUNNEL CAPTAINS

The ships' masters were the heroes, or the villains, of the day. Taking ultimate responsibility for all that went on aboard the steamers, their position was very much in the public gaze, and literally so, for none of the Campbell paddle steamers ever had even a wheelhouse to shelter their deck-officers from the public, let alone the elements. By the end of each season, we all shared the same weather-worn complexion. Here follows an insider's thumbnail sketch of each of the post-War captains.

FINDLEY BRANDER had been brought down from the Clyde by the Campbells twenty years before the War. He was in charge of *Glen Usk*. He loved the ferry service between Cardiff and Weston. On the other hand, the Ilfracombe run was bad news.

BERT MURPHY went minesweeping with P.&A.C. ships during the War. Afterwards, he was master of *Glen Gower, Cardiff Queen* then *Britannia*. When on the Swansea run, Bert's pet aversion was berthing at Porthcawl. He was a nice man, and a pretty fearless ship-handler.

JOE PHILLIPS was another survivor of the wartime paddlers, and became master of *Glen Gower, Britannia* and *Bristol Queen*. He was rather apprehensive and unsure of his own undoubted ability as a good shiphandler.

Gentleman Best Murphy in his anti-Napoleon stance.

BILL WATSON was also ex-RNR. A pre-War master in Campbells, he had a yo-yo peacetime career in the company, but found his niche in the Navy, and was suitably decorated for his services there. He was sunk on *Brighton Queen* at Dunkirk. Bill survived; many didn't. His hobby was buying and selling antiques, and he set many profitable courses between the salerooms of Bristol, often using his innate ability to influence values at auction previews to

Bill Watson, a great 'yo-yo' character, seen here lying down on the job.

advantage, helped by his 'discovery' of suspected woodworm on choice items. Bill ended his colourful career as 'purser' on the Clifton Suspension Bridge.

ARCHIE HARRIS was marine superintendent and another RNR transferee from P.&A.C. when the War started. He was master of many of the ships before and after the War, including *Cardiff Queen* and *Britannia*. Despite the end of general hostilities in 1945, they continued unabated between Harris and Watson.

LACHLAN McLEAN SHEDDEN was another P.&A.C. ex-RNR Captain. He was master of *Ravenswood* in 1948, after delivering *Cardiff Queen* from Scottish builders in 1947. He was a solid seaman from the Isle of Iona. He left to join the Avonmouth Dock Pilots.

1955 masters:
(from top and left)
Jack George, *Bristol Queen*;
George Gunn, *Cardiff Queen*;
Bert Murphy, *Britannia*;
Jack Harris, *Glen Gower*;
Leo Virgo, *Glen Usk*;
Archie Harris, shore superintendent.

Archie is saying to the photographer 'Hurry up and take this picture, I can see Watson coming along the deck.'

BILL COUVES was master of *Empress Queen*, and a pre-War P.&A.C. man. His shiphandling was never in doubt, neither was his lack of diplomacy!

TOM KIDD was engaged by Campbells to take over as master of *Empress Queen* after a season on the South Coast as 'makee learn' with Couves. Tom was not really interested in Bristol Channel paddle steamers. When Campbells decided *Empress Queen* was surplus to requirements, so too was Captain Kidd.

GEORGE GUNN. As the author of this book it is necessary to include myself at this stage, being the first newcomer to the Company to be appointed Master of a paddle-steamer after the War. At 27 years old, I was probably the youngest. Perhaps it wasn't the daunting situation it should have been, and no doubt there were others who were more worried about it than me. Of course in 1950 with ten years' sea time behind me, nothing *seemed* difficult.

LEO VIRGO worked on early White Funnel ships as a boy before the War. Like Captain George, he then went to sea, and obtained his certificates. When I re-joined *Ravenswood* from *Britannia* in 1953 Leo was mate of the ship. When I left there in February 1954 he took over as master.

NEVILLE COTTMAN served his time as an apprentice pilot with the Bristol Pilotage Authority. He was a good mate when I had him on *Cardiff Queen*. He didn't always see eye-to-eye with the management of the Company, and was not averse to making it known. Going ashore at the Horseshoe Bend in the River Avon was the ultimate bad experience on an ebbing tide, which everyone dreaded. Neville experienced this in 1959 on *Glen Usk*. Passengers were taken up

The author, 1952. The feeding couldn't have been very good on board *Ravenswood* that year.

Leo in non-aggressive stance.

the steep face of the bank to the Portway. There were no casualties, and *Glen Usk* survived physically. The inevitable criticism ensued, that the ship should not have left Bristol so late on the tide. Only the master can make that decision. Many have taken the risk and have come through unscathed; on this occasion Neville gambled and lost.

JACK HARRIS was mate on *Glen Gower* when I relieved Joe Phillips in 1950, my first command. His knowledge of the ship and his vast experience as master of coastal vessels before joining Campbells were invaluable. He was a coasting man; I was still a 'deep sea' sailor, but learning fast. Jack helped a lot in my initiation. He became master of *Glen Gower* and started the no-passport trips to France.

JACK GEORGE—'CAPTAIN OF THE QUEEN'. Jack George started with Campbells as a chocolate boy on their very early pre-War ships. He sailed the Atlantic with Bristol City Line until he obtained his Foreign-Going Master's ticket. He was in charge of the turbine-steamer *Empress Queen* during the War and *Bristol Queen* thereafter.

Jack was a legend in his own time. No-one else had his length of experience or knew every inch of the Bristol Channel the way he did. He was also a consummate ship-handler, and, when he had a chief engineer he could rely on to give bridge-control-like engine movements, could do things with a paddle steamer that left the rest of us gasping in his wake. The following is an extract from the 1964 Bristol Channel Guide:-

> Captain Jack George, the best known shipmaster in the Bristol Channel with the longest service ever in charge of Bristol Channel ships, is now in his 38th year in command of P.& A. Campbell's

Jack George, 1956. Always instructable, but when he took out his pocket watch and rubbed the face of it, there was sure to be something not right with time or tide.

vessels. During these 38 years this has included *Cambria*, *Westward Ho*, *Glen Usk*, *Britannia*, *Empress Queen* and now *Bristol Queen*. Which of these fine ships was his favourite? Ask him that question and I doubt whether you will receive a definite answer. Each ship has a special meaning to him. But there's one name which may be mentioned more than others, *Britannia*.

Was *Britannia* the fastest vessel ever to sail under the famous White Funnels? Captain George can tell of remarkable passages made by this ship, certainly never bettered, and no doubt will remain so until hovercraft services are established.

This amazing man joined Campbells in 1906 as a boy in the catering department, and after a short time there, went to sea on deck in foreign-going ships. In due course he obtained a Master's Certificate and returned to his first love as Chief Officer in the passenger steamers in 1923. 1926 saw his promotion to master and the start of an outstanding career. He has been in charge of *Bristol Queen* since 1948 and will no doubt finish his unique career with P.& A. Campbell as master of their finest ship.

The above is taken from one of three *Bristol Channel Guides* I had published in the early 'sixties for sale on the piers and the ships. They sold then for 1/6d (7.5p), included advertisements, and at the end of the season they gave them to the children. They were very basic, but sold well in the absence of anything else. The P.&A. advertising guru thought it was a good idea, and produced a Company handbook with no adverts priced 3/6d (17.5p). It was very costly to produce, there were practically no sales at that price and it lost money all round. So much for sophistication!

PHILLIP POWER joined Campbells in June 1957. His first appointment to a ship was as 'makee learn' mate on *Cardiff Queen*. The first I knew of Phil was when he came on board at Porthcawl. He stayed with us for about three weeks. He must have liked it, as he spent the next 13 years sailing Campbell's ships

Phillip Power, 1965.

around the Bristol and English Channels. Apart from being master of *Cardiff Queen* and *Bristol Queen*, Phil did stints on *St.Trillo*, *Westward Ho* and *Balmoral*, before joining Barry Harbour Pilots in 1970. As a Campbell master, he became well-loved for his often audible commentaries from the bridge on matters of navigational interest. He was—and still is—a very skilful ship-handler, and succeeded more often than most in getting paddle steamers alongside piers in seemingly impossible weather conditions. Eventually he 'swallowed the anchor', and now lives a more peaceful life in retirement in Penarth.

JACK WIDE was a pre-War master of White Funnel Steamers. Jack became piermaster and director of the Weston Pier Company—a very flourishing business before the Severn Bridge opened. A full turn of the wheel found Jack an employee once more of Campbells. They bought Weston Pier, and Captain Wide went to sea again, on the Dover Cross-Channel Hovercraft Service. Jack Wide had a square rig master's certificate, a foreign-going master's certificate for steam and motor ships, and if Townsend had continued to operate hovercraft, he would have qualified for a hovercraft pilot's

Jack Wide

licence. They pulled out of it after two years. Jack Wide's qualifications could never possibly have been equalled. Roland Wickenden, Chairman of European Ferries, is reputed to have said that hovercraft in the English Channel would never be a financially viable form of competition to passenger ferries. He hasn't been proved very far wrong. Of course, he seldom ever was. After the hovercraft interlude, Jack Wide returned to Weston Pier and then did some stints as relief master of *Cardiff Queen* and *Bristol Queen*. In fact he was the last master of both these ships, being full-time on *Cardiff Queen* in 1966 (her last year) and relieving master on *Bristol Queen* when she was withdrawn from service. This happened after her port paddle wheel took a turn for the worse off Barry in late August 1967. The official Company line was that she had hit a submerged object. Jack, in private, was not of that opinion. A few weeks before, in an attempt to cure the persistent cracking of the ship's new paddle-floats which had been fitted the previous winter, reinforcing plates were welded over the floats where they were bolted on to the brackets. This meant that, instead of shaped one-inch thick pieces of steel hitting the water as each float entered it, three-inch thick pieces of steel struck the water. In addition, the ship's regular engineers, sensing what was going to happen, had all left, and *Bristol Queen* was at the mercy of inexperienced engineers who did little if any wheel-maintenance. 'Something had to give', Jack said. 'The whole bloody wheel did.' Thus came about the tragic end of one of the last and finest of all paddle steamers. Had she survived just a few more years into the 'preservation era', we would probably still be sailing around the coast in her.

Bristol Queen, with Jack George as captain and Leo Virgo as mate, arriving at Ilfracombe.

The original officers of *Britannia*. Captain Dan Taylor (far right of front row) succeeded captain Peter Campbell (front centre) as master of *Britannia*.

WHITE FUNNEL GUV'NORS

CAPTAIN PETER CAMPBELL, known as the 'Old Guv'nor' even long after his death, had a greater influence on the Company than any other. He was exceptional in having both a master's and a chief engineer's certificate. He had virtually been brought up on the bridges of paddle steamers in his father's Clyde fleet of White Funnel Holy Loch steamers. It was his influence above all that made the White Funnel Fleet legendary in terms of the quality of its steamers, their meticulous upkeep, and the high standards of passenger service provided from the beginning of the Bristol Channel service in 1887 almost up until the advent of the second world war. Even in my time with the company in the 1950s, the influence of the Old Guv'nor was not hard to find.

W.G. BANKS succeeded Peter Campbell in 1938, and saw the Company through into the early 1950's. An engineer by trade, his most notable contribution was perhaps the design of the patent Campbell and Banks piston-rings, which were a feature of the Spitfire aircraft and which were subsequently fitted to all Campbell's steamers. His son, **BILL BANKS**, took over after the War, and was joint Managing Director with Clifton Smith-Cox between 1952 and 1954.

SYDNEY CLIFTON SMITH-COX joined Campbell's board in 1952, became joint managing director with Bill Banks, and took over in 1954. His intervention came at a crucial time. There had only been two or three good trading years since the War and it was becoming clear that something had to be done to keep the company's head above water. It wasn't sufficient to keep hoping that next year's summer would be better than the last. The survival history of pre-War passenger companies in the Bristol Channel wasn't good. Campbells were the sole survivors, although there were opinions that war came along at the right time.

Sydney Clifton Smith-Cox

The reformed Company in 1946 started with great expectations, but by the time Smith-Cox took over it was apparently heading for problems. A question frequently asked was, 'Was it wrong to build paddle steamers after the War when the money could have been used for more economical twin-screw diesel ships?'

Passengers then were happy to enjoy the freedom of movement lost during the War years, and it didn't matter much what type of vessel gave them a good day out. The significance of the paddle-steamer era hadn't yet sunk in.

Smith-Cox's intervention kept the Fleet afloat, and maintained services for many years. His motivation was a determination to succeed, and a lifelong love of the ships and the company. I first met him by accident, during winter lay-up in 1949. My bicycle almost knocked him over on Mardyke Quay. 'You're mate of this *Bristol Queen* here, aren't you? I hope you can navigate better than ride that bicycle.'

I must have at one time criticised the condition of the hat he wore on the ships, for it had a hole in the peak. These comments were relayed by 'galley wireless' it seems, and one day, he bounded aboard *Bristol Queen*, came on the bridge and said 'Mr Gunn, I believe you have been making derogatory remarks about my hat. Well you'll be pleased to hear it blew over the side on *Glen Usk* last week'.

Smith-Cox's contribution to the operation of the company wasn't popular with everyone. Some of the old hands resented changes, of which there were many. It was felt there was a general lowering of the high standards Campbells had set before the War and tried to continue in the following years. Unfortunately economics and the cost of survival didn't allow much else. I worked with S-C. for over twenty years and respected what he was attempting to do. If success was based on personal effort only, he couldn't possibly have failed, but unfortunately it isn't.

Clifton Smith-Cox was very down-to-earth in every way. He hated snobbery. He was a pint-of-bitter man, although occasionally he did have a gin and french. Roy Boucher, chairman of Campbells, was also chairman of Bristol United Brewery. His company had devised a system similar to the American Automat where beer could be dispensed without the aid of barmaids or barmen. Smith-Cox declared war on the scheme and vowed not a drop of Bristol United Best Bitter, or anything else similarly purveyed, would pass his lips. 'George', he said, 'It's not only the principle of the thing, but can you imagine standing around, looking at four walls drinking a pint of beer, with no attractive barmaids serving it?' I couldn't have agreed more.

CHOCOLATE BOY TO CHIEF STEWARD

SYD GRAY, probably the only former Campbell Chocolate Boy still around, started work on *Britannia* in 1934 at the age of thirteen. Another, but much earlier holder of the same position, was then master of the ship, Captain Jack George.

First of all Syd was a 'Sunday and Bank Holiday Boy'. He wore a FRY'S peaked cap, carried a leather cash shoulder-bag, a tray filled with Fry's and Cadbury's products, White Funnel Sailing Guides, and Campbell's badges. When he progressed to full time the weekly wage of 5/- (25p) plus tips and meals, and the freedom to wander round the ship and enjoy the trip, were 'great'.

At the age of fifteen Syd joined *Britannia* as dining saloon cashier. This was a very responsible job for a boy of his age. He supplied both bars and the Chocolate Boys with cigarettes and chocs, taking their money and running the saloon cash-desk bar for the waiters. He also took the cash for meals served in the saloon. At the same age Syd was introduced to the skills necessary to make a good barman. The learning process involved dispensing every kind of drink, and knowing what to recommend when asked. His knowledge of wines, spirits, champagnes, beers, soft drinks and cocktails, all learned at this early age, stood him in good stead throughout the rest of a very long catering career ashore and afloat.

When it is said 'I used to work 24 hours a day', this could have applied to Campbell's pre-War. Although a few hours in the 24 were allocated for sleeping purposes, these were frequently far from restful. Syd's bunk was in the 'Glory Hole', a compartment situated underneath the after mooring-capstan. A tick pillow and two blankets were Company issue; individuals supplied their own mattresses. These were made of gunny filled with straw, and well-known in British ships of the day as Donkeys' Breakfasts. Syd bought his at Rice's Ironmongers, Hotwells Road, and walked on board the ship with it over his head. The price was 2/6d (12.5p). Carrying his Donkey's Breakfast aboard was a

special moment. He had signed on the Ship's Articles of Agreement as a full member of the crew for the first time.

During five years of war, Syd sailed in the catering departments of merchant ships, and ultimately joined Captain George as ordinary seaman on *Empress Queen* ferrying troops between Scotland and Ireland.

Syd and I first sailed together on *Bristol Queen* in 1949. He was a barman with Reg Tyrell as chief steward. I was chief officer with Jack George. Eventually we sailed together on other vessels, and remained good friends, colleagues, and close neighbours for years. Few have heard of Campbells United football team, a brainchild of Gray and Gunn. We formed a team from the ships, the office, and the Underfall Yard. Roger Whyte, second engineer on *Ravenswood* and a fully-fit rugby player, was goalkeeper. He was the busiest man on the field picking the ball out of the net (when there was a net). We played at Clifton Down, Long Ashton and other venues against selected teams. The final match was against Stoke Park Colony, away. Syd Gray even now refuses to accept any

Syd Gray.

responsibility for our 10-0 defeat. He was injured and tried to help the best he could by acting as a linesman. Even his slightly biased decisions were of no avail. We discovered too late that the Colony players spent most of their leisure-time playing football. That defeat was the end of the football-season, and of Campbell's United.

Another stage in Syd Gray's career with Campbell's was when he worked on *Bristol Queen* at the fitting-out stage. *Bristol Queen* was a worthy successor to *Britannia* as the 'Bristol Boat', the traditional flagship of the fleet, and she was considered by many to be the best of all paddle steamers. She was a fine example of traditional Bristol shipbuilding, and a credit to shipbuilders Charles Hills. Every item of a ship's construction and fitting out has its own significance and importance. Even Toilet Seats.

Mr Banks, Managing Director, on an inspection of the new ship, was told by Syd that the builders had fitted ladies' seats instead of gents' seats in the gents' toilets. 'What do you mean gents' seats?' Syd said to him, 'They have a hygiene gap in the front of them.' 'Oh, do they?' said Banks. The M.D. was later heard berating the yard foreman, 'Don't you know the difference between ladies' and gents' toilet seats? Well if you don't, find out and change them accordingly.' Everyone can be an expert in something.

WHITE FUNNEL SHIPS

I deal here with the ships, and my memories of them, in the order in which I came across them in my time as chief officer and master.

RAVENSWOOD. Built on the Clyde in 1891 for the new Campbell Bristol Channel venture. Length 215ft. Beam 24ft. Re-engined in 1909. Served in both World Wars. Scrapped 1955. Speed—variable up to 13 knots.

Paddle Steamer *Ravenswood,* built in 1891, and my first Campbell ship, was the first ship Campbells built new for the Bristol Channel. She was withdrawn from service in 1955. A survivor of naval duties in two World Wars, she returned from both to resume her rôle as the little workhorse of the fleet. By the time I joined her in 1948, steel had replaced almost all her original iron shell-plating, and many other structural- and design-changes had been made to the ship. Everyone

Ravenswood on an afternoon cruise from Newport to Bristol, on a neap tide, May 1952. Master: George Gunn; mate: Les Brooks.

who had the experience of taking an active part in sailing *Ravenswood*, whether on deck or in the engine-room, felt great affection for the ship: she was something very special. Working for just one season on *Ravenswood* would provide memories of events unlikely to happen elsewhere during a sea-going career. She became a firm favourite with me, and if anyone asks me now which of the White Funnel paddlers held prime place in my affections, *Ravenswood* is the one.

Ravenswood was a good ship in the rivers. What she lacked in speed and comfort she made up for in nostalgia, being the first purpose-built White Funnel Bristol Channel paddler. She was very popular in Newport, especially with the Boys' Brigade. *Ravenswood* carried the Newport Boys' Brigade Troop to Weston year after year for their annual camp. The only casualty sustained was one kitbag, which was aimed from the pier to the paddle-box and missed. It was last seen doing about five knots down-Channel past Birnbeck Island. The weather on this trip was particularly bad. We had several attempts to get alongside, and

Ravenswood 1948. On a leisurely afternoon cruise along the Welsh coast from Barry. Filling in time until water at Weston to resume the Ferry service for the evening. Master: Lachlan McLean Shedder.

eventually made it. Being an old Boys' Brigade boy myself, the presentation of a 'Sure & Steadfast' plaque for services rendered in 1952 is a cherished memento of *Ravenswood*'s ability to make Weston Pier under conditions where others wouldn't.

Ravenswood's speed was variable according to circumstances, which included steam pressure, coal, firemen, tidal assistance or otherwise. She wasn't called 'The Scratcher' for nothing, and in order to keep time, had to scrape over sandbanks to get in and out of piers and berths, when other ships weren't expected to. There was no better boost to a master's confidence than to be on schedule after a full day's sailings with *Ravenswood*.

From morning to night nothing had to be taken for granted. The challenges *Ravenswood* presented were not for the faint-hearted. There is no better way to learn than the hard way. In Campbells, that was the *Ravenswood* way.

Ravenswood was quick on the helm and engines. As long as she sailed in the upper reaches of the Channel, all would be fine. Apart from one Briton Ferry trip, Minehead was my furthest *Ravenswood* 'voyage'.

After my first spell on her in 1948, a second appointment came early in July 1952. I was sent by Captain Archie Harris, marine superintendent, to Newport to take over from Captain Bill Watson. He said, 'Watson has made a fool of himself again.' Under the circumstances, there were misgivings about meeting Bill on board. They proved unnecessary. He and his niece were busy packing and he seemed quite undisturbed at losing his job again. He wished me the best of luck with my new command and left the ship.

Nobody will be surprised that steam played a part in that story. Steam pervaded *Ravenswood*'s activities from time to time. Events leading up to Bill's departure were covered in the *South Wales Argus*, and are worth recording, as the following extract from the paper shows:-

STOKER GAOLED AT NEWPORT ENDANGERED PADDLE STEAMER TRYING TO SAVE HIMSELF WORK. Because he wanted to keep to a minimum the ashes he would have to clear, a stoker on board the paddle steamer Ravenswood did not keep the boiler's furnace burning properly. The result was the steam pressure fell and when 'Full Steam Ahead' was ordered as the vessel was steaming up the River Usk from Weston to Newport on Monday evening the instruction could not be executed. The stoker was reprimanded, and in reply assaulted the second engineer. This was stated at Newport Magistrates' Court where the stoker George Bernard Higgins was sent to prison for five months. Of this sentence, three months was 'for refusing to do a lawful act proper and requisite for preserving the ship from damage', and two months for 'assaulting the second engineer'. On the trip the second engineer went down to the stokehold and told Higgins to get a good head of steam. He refused to carry out the order, followed the engineer up on deck, struck him a heavy blow over the bridge of the nose, cutting and damaging his eye. Alexander Campbell of Bristol, Chief Engineer, stated that a minimum pressure of 110 lbs of steam was needed for the safety of the ship, but on this occasion it had dropped to 90 lbs. Questioned by the defendant, the witness agreed that the ship had once been brought into port with a pressure of only 75 lbs but added 'however only just'.

Roy Boucher, a prominent Bristol businessman and solicitor, was chairman of Campbells at that time. He had made the arrangements for legal representation of the company's case, and appointed the barrister. Witnesses were Alex Campbell, chief engineer; R. Smith, second engineer; and Captain Bill Watson.

Prior to presenting himself at court, Bill had spent some time socialising with his friend the landlord of the Isca public house. At the pre-hearing briefing the barrister decided that Bill's testimony would not advantage the company's case against the accused. He informed Roy Boucher, hence my speedy transfer from mate of *Bristol Queen* to master of *Ravenswood*—my first permanent Campbell command.

Ravenswood was the first steamer to call at the new Ilfracombe Pier on 31st May 1952, and apart from a memorable charter trip from Briton Ferry to Weston-Super-Mare on 26th June 1948, I can't recall other down-Channel passages made by her between these dates.

The Briton Ferry event had required both *Glen Gower* and *Ravenswood* to carry the members of the Briton Ferry Working Mens' Club and their families for their day out. *Glen Gower* departed first; we followed with the balance of the passengers on *Ravenswood*.

Captain Murphy on *Glen Gower* went down inside through the Nash Passage. Captain Shedden on *Ravenswood* opted to go outside to try to take advantage of the remainder of the flood tide. It wasn't a good option, and became worse when the firemen couldn't maintain steam. *Glen Gower* receded into the distance. When the ebb started to set against *Ravenswood* it became obvious to some of the more knowledgeable passengers that all was not well, and that they might not get to Weston in time for the lunch ashore. Questions and comments floated up from the deck. I discovered then how vulnerable *Ravenswood*'s little wooden navigating bridge was under siege.

An important job on this ship was lavatory-attendant, particularly in bad weather or when short of steam. On this occasion Stanley's services were required in the stokehold to help supply the firemen with sufficient coal to raise enough steam to get to Weston at all on that tide. The gents' toilets had to survive under their own steam for the rest of that passage. It was every man for himself. We scraped into Weston on the very last of the tide. On the return passage that evening, everyone wanted to board *Glen Gower*, and it was only for want of space that *Ravenswood* had any passengers at all.

The photograph on p. 13 of Captain Peter Campbell (the Old Guv'nor) on the bridge of Ravenswood—which was the first new ship he had built for passenger operations in the Bristol Channel—shows the famous brass steering wheel. Although many other original features of the ship were drstically altered during 65 years of continuous service, including two world wars with the Royal Navy, the 'old scratcher's' wheel was there until the end.

I have often been asked, 'Does the captain steer the ship?' The answer is always 'No, it's usually able seamen and quartermasters.' However in Campbells, unlike most other steamship companies, all close quarter steering was done by the mate. This included up and down rivers, in and out of harbours and approaching and going alongside piers and pontoon berths. A busy day on short passages between Cardiff, Penarth and Weston with a trip up the Usk or Avon, saw the mate almost continually at the wheel. At these times only he and the captain were on the bridge. This was considered to create a close understanding between them for efficient handling of the ship, and the best learning process for an aspiring master. Handling the old ships with their large steering wheels and chain and rod steering gear was quite different to the new

Ravenswood going 'Full Out' to catch a tide. 'With the wind'.

ones and their hydraulic Telemotor systems. Ravenswood, perhaps more than the other two coal burners, had to be coaxed and cajoled to get her alongside awkward berths like Weston under difficult weather and tidal conditions. It was frequently hard going for 'the man at the wheel'. One year as mate of Ravenswood working in the upper reches of the Bristol Channel proved the point.

Approaching Weston Pier near the end of season 1948 I had the wheel hard a' starboard trying to keep the ship up to the tidal set and close into the face of the landing stage when Shedden frantically shouted 'Hard a' port, mate! The damned tide's changed again.' I pulled and pushed the wheel through its full sequence to try to avert what then

appeared to be imminent disaster. There was a sudden painful feeling in the third finger left hand. My gold signet ring had worn right through after five months continuous contact with Ravenswood's brass wheel and the two ends were now embedded in the finger.

There was no better way to get to know your own ship than steering her through 'thick and thin'. Extreme wind and weather effects on the rudder were transmitted through the system up to the bridge to the man at the wheel. This 'first hand' information was not so readily available on the newer and more sophisticated ships, and contributed a bit more to a new mate's learning processes. It's an ill wind . . .

BRISTOL QUEEN. Built in 1946 by Charles Hill & Sons, Bristol. The first of two new buildings to replace ships lost during the War. Length 245ft. Beam 31ft. Speed 18 knots.

Hills could easily claim that in *Bristol Queen* they had built the finest vessel of her class. Few would argue about that. Those who had sailed on her for any length of time would certainly agree.

With Captain Jack George on the bridge and Jack Giles, chief engineer, at the engine-controls *Bristol Queen* was at her best, and never bettered, before or after. Coming directly to *B.Q.* as mate in 1949 after sculling around the Channel in *Ravenswood* was quite a culture shock. The daily service from Bristol on the Flagship was different. Until I arrived, the best officers and men usually manned *Bristol Queen*. Jack George, Jack Giles, chief steward Reg Tyrell, purser Bill Berry, head barman Syd Gray, and Harold the bosun. It was said that Harold could throw a heaving line across the Bristol Channel. I can't remember him ever being called on to do so. Jack brought the ship in so fast and close to the piers that Harold often just had to pass the line straight into the hands of the mooring gang. Although *Bristol Queen* was a fine ship, well-built, and suitable for most coastal work around the British Isles, all wasn't, in my opinion, perfect. That standard of ship hasn't yet been achieved. I didn't like the bridge, where we spent most of our time. Unlike *Cardiff Queen*'s well laid-out teakwood compact unit, *Bristol Queen*'s bridge lacked character in the design, and this wasn't helped by accommodating passengers on the after end, who 'breathed down your neck' when you were working the ship. Some of Campbell's paddle steamers would have benefited from having a wheelhouse, none more so than *Bristol Queen*. She was still a wonderful vessel.

Bristol Queen returning from her trials, 9 September, 1946.

EMPRESS QUEEN Built by Ailsa Shipbuilding Co., Troon, 1939. Turbine twin-screw. Length 270ft. Beam 37ft. Speed 17 knots.

Campbells' first departure from paddle steamers was this large twin-screw turbine-vessel. She was also the largest disappointment of any vessel in the Company's history. Built by Ailsa in Troon, *Empress Queen* was intended to provide revolutionary standards of comfort on no-passport day-trips to France. The ship never had the chance to prove it. By the time she was ready for sea the War had started. The ship was commissioned by the Admiralty, re-named *Queen Eagle* and, with other vessels, carried troops between Scotland and Northern Ireland. Captain Jack George was given command, and continued in that role for some time after the War ended, while sailing in the Bristol Channel. *Empress Queen* proved to be unsuitable here, and was switched to cruising on the South Coast of England. That had limited success, and after one subsequent season of day-trips between Torquay and the Channel Islands, the ship was laid up again at Bristol city centre. The fight by Campbells to get Government approval for cross-Channel day-trips to France took longer than expected, and by the time it happened, *Empress Queen* had been sold to the Greeks. The only ship available by then for the trips to France was *Glen Gower*, which was quite unsuitable for the job.

Empress Queen's first cruise from Swansea, 1947.

On the other hand, Captain Kavonides, who bought *Empress Queen* for about £30,000, made his best-ever investment. He re-named the ship *Phillipos*, changed her from turbine to diesel, fitted cabin-accommodation, and operated her on cruises in the Mediterranean and Black Sea. *Phillipos* was the foundation of his post-War fleet of cruise-ships, and became one of Piraeus's best-known and popular passenger vessels. During the 1960s when I was a Swansea Harbour Pilot, we handled more Greek-registered ships than any other foreign nationality. I often asked masters of them if the ship was still sailing out there. I can't remember any of them saying 'Who's *Phillipos*?' They all knew her.

Having carried out the Sale & Purchase drydocking of the ship at Avonmouth, and looked after her in Bristol prior to and during the take-over, I had got to know Kavonides, his shipmaster and his crew, when they eventually joined to take her away.

It was my first experience of Greek business acumen. *Empress Queen* was sold to them in operating condition, fully fitted out. Even the turbines hadn't long been re-bladed at enormous cost to the Company. A regular inventory of everything on board was taken, usually by one or

other of the pursers working during the winter months. Kavonides and his men went through everything with a fine toothcomb. Two items were missing from his list. The first of these was the ship's bell outside the front of the wheelhouse. An *Empress Queen* bell suitably inscribed had to be supplied. The second item was more problematic. On British merchant ships during the War, all lifeboats were fitted out with galvanised food-, water-, and equipment-tanks, which were secured by metal bands and slung underneath the thwarts of the lifeboats. This practice stopped when the War finished on certain classes of ships, and these tanks were removed. Sometime in the interim period they had been removed from *Empress Queen*, but were still on the ship's equipment inventory. Tanks of a similar type had to be supplied and fitted before the deal could be completed, even though there was no requirement for them on this ship.

When I joined the crew of *Empress Queen* in 1950, my progression up until then had been *Ravenswood* 1948, *Bristol Queen* 1949, *Empress Queen* 1950. Captain Tom Kidd was then in command of the ship, I was his chief officer, and we sailed for the South Coast. Our first berthing

The Sale and Purchase dry docking of *Empress Queen* at Avonmouth, 1955.

Empress Queen in 1947 when Jack George was master of the ship.

was Brighton Palace Pier to start the season. This was the usual courtesy call, to meet the people, then on to Newhaven where we laid up each night after the day's sailings. Tom Kidd was on the telegraphs, I was at the wheel. He put the engines half astern as we were approaching the landing area, but nothing happened. Then full astern. The reception party were by then being passed to port. It was a beautiful summer's day. Brighton Beach was busy, and swimmers were in abundance, some making for the ship, but not for long. Captain Kidd said 'Hard a' starboard' and put both engines full speed ahead. *Empress Queen* for the first time responded immediately—and so did the swimmers, pursued by a monster wave. Luckily, it was high water. When we regrouped outside, Tom Kidd said 'That's the first and last time I'll do it that way', and it was. The incident was reported in the press the following day, with very favourable comments on the Captain's reactions, under the circumstances.

Although it was very enjoyable being chief officer of such a fine ship as *Empress Queen*, it was always clear it required cross-Channel trips, as cruising up and down the coast was wasteful. We sailed from Brighton, Eastbourne, Hastings, Southampton, and around the Isle of Wight, and every other possible combination of coastal cruising of which the ship was capable. *Empress Queen* was too big, too expensive to run, and too good for the job. Too frequently, we were informed the weather conditions were unsuitable for her at one or other of the piers. The smaller, much lighter paddle steamers wouldn't have had these messages. There seemed to be plenty of time for us to play tennis, or pitch and putt at the course overlooked by Roedean School. Evening visits to Seaford for a beer and a game of darts were frequently on the agenda.

With the alternative landing-faces, Brighton Pier was almost always available. Eastbourne was sometimes willing to accept the ship under doubtful conditions. Hastings landing stage at the end of the Pier was considered to be well-sprung and sympathetic to a bit of impact. Captain Couves, on one occasion going alongside Hastings with *Empress Queen,* got little sympathy from the Pier, and none from Troise and His Mandoliers. Their musical recital was dramatically terminated by the force of the ship's arrival.

36

GLEN USK. **Built in 1914 by Ailsa Shipbuilders, Troon. Length 224ft. Beam 28ft. Speed 15 knots. Served in both World Wars.**

The last of the fleet to be released by the Navy after the War, *Glen Usk* was generally the first ship out at Easter, and the last to finish at the end of the season. She carried on the Cardiff to Weston service into the autumn. Captain Findley Brander was her master for a number of years after the War. He was one of the Old Guv'nor's original Scottish contingent, and stayed on board the ship summer and winter, living in a rather reclusive manner. He went home for a couple of weeks every year, around Christmas and New Year. *Glen Usk* was always associated with the Ferry, and ploughed back and forth there day after day. From time to time *Glen Usk* had to make a trip down-Channel to Ilfracombe. Brander would say, 'I'm going down there again tomorrow. It's too much for the wee boat.' He didn't like it.

By the 1950s, *Glen Usk*, *Ravenswood*, and to some extent *Glen Gower*, the three ageing coal-burners, didn't perform well on longer passages. Keeping a full head of steam could be a problem. This was much less evident on short runs with frequent periods alongside. Good coal firemen were becoming scarce, and many of those available weren't so keen on the labour involved in keeping old coal burners 'on the mark'.

Bunkering the three oil-fired paddle steamers at Cardiff was relatively easy. The oil was run from a storage tank at the top of the ramp into the ships by gravity. Coal bunkering was very different. Jack and his merry men wheeled huge barrows of coal loaded from rail-trucks down the ramps and up into the ships every night. Just pushing one of the empty barrows back up to the truck was beyond the average person. Many tried it without success. Jack inherited the job. He regularly said 'This job killed my father, but it's not going to kill me.'

One very well documented moment of drama for *Glen Usk* was in 1959 when she went ashore at the Horseshoe Bend on the River Avon, when passengers had to be evacuated. Fortunately no one was harmed.

Glen Usk, 1948-9: master, Findley Brander; mate, Dave Miles.

Glen Usk askore in the River Avon, the passengers having been safely landed.

The snapshot of the officers in conference is a telling one! I would guess that Jim Keating, the purser, is probably preparing the defence: 'They're going to say we shouldn't have left Bristol so late on tide, so this is what I would do about it . . .' Neville Coltman, the captain, is not quite convinced. The engineer, meanwhile, rolls his own.

Blowing off steam as low water approaches.

Jim the purser, ready for action, awaits the tell-tale bubble to show she is afloat once more.

GLEN GOWER. Built in 1922 by Ailsa Shipbuilders, Troon. Length 235ft. Beam 28ft. Served in World War Two. Speed 15 knots.

Glen Gower was the first and only Campbells steamer to be built specifically for the Swansea service, and ran from there for a number of years before the War. She re-opened the South-Coast-of-England service in 1947, but was replaced there after a short period of time by the turbine *Empress Queen*. In 1948 and 1949 *Glen Gower* went back to her rightful station at Swansea, being replaced in 1950 by *Cardiff Queen*. I joined *Glen Gower* at Weston in 1950. This was my first command, relieving Captain Joe Phillips for a few weeks. It didn't take long to discover some of this ship's obstinate features. The first passage was from Weston, up the River Usk at night. At the *Ravenswoo*d's usual position down below the berth at Newport Bridge, it was hard a' starboard and full ahead on the engines to get her bow round to stick in the mud and swing to the flood tide. *Glen Gower* didn't respond like *Ravenswood*, and many engine-movements later brought up alongside a disused jetty on the other side of the river. There were still two hours of flood tide. We couldn't move until after high water when the ebb tide started. It was a long two hours for us. It was much longer for the two hundred passengers who couldn't get ashore for their transport home. In 1950, passengers travelled to the ships by bus, train, or shank's pony. The era of the car and parking for the day was still some way off.

The fate of an earlier P.& A. ship *Bonnie Doon* was always in mind when swinging below Newport Bridge on the flood tide. She got into similar difficulties , but didn't get out of it so easily, and ended up

Glen Gower in 1949: master, Bert Murphy; mate, Jimmy Martin.

impaled across the parapets of the bridge. The ship was there for some time, and was subjected to certain actions from the street above, which are best left to the imagination. With *Glen Gower*, it never happened again. The ship's sluggish reactions were taken into account.

CARDIFF QUEEN. Built by Fairfields, Govan, in 1947. Length 240ft. Beam 30ft. Speed 17 knots.

Cardiff Queen was the last paddle-steamer built for Campbells, being new in 1947. I was fortunate to be master of her for five of the more halcyon years—1954 to 1958. I had previous spells as mate in 1950 and 1951. Most of our work during these years was on the Swansea station, known as the bad weather run. It certainly lived up to its reputation.

I joined the ship in Swansea on 21st August 1950, after a period as master relieving Captain Joe Phillips on *Glen Gower*. The regular mate of *Cardiff Queen* then was Jimmy Martin, who had more than fifty years as mate of paddle steamers behind him. He came to P.&A. with the acquisition of Barry Railway ships in 1911. He never sailed as master of a ship. I was there to get qualifying time in for a Swansea Pilotage Licence. Captain Bert Murphy was in charge of the ship at that time.

The first day of real drama came less than a month later. On 16th September 1950, after arriving at Ilfracombe, the weather deteriorated and the return trip to Swansea was cancelled. *Cardiff Queen* tied up in the Harbour inside the Pier at Stone Bench, and took the bottom at the next low water. All was peaceful for a few hours until the tide started to make again. When the ship started to lift off the bottom, the heavy surge of the sea coming into the harbour parted all of the ropes except one six-inch aft. This rope was always the last one to be let go, used to swing the stern of the vessel round the pier. Syd Leonard the chief engineer and his crew did a great job getting enough steam in less than twenty minutes to turn the engines. We hacked the rope off the bits and at that time *Cardiff Queen* was at the mercy of the elements. The wind had strengthened and with the very limited engine power available was too close to the rocks for comfort. The southerly wind blew the ship into the channel just clear. Even with more steam the ship was difficult to

manage, but eventually was turned round and headed east, running before the strongest wind I had ever seen in the Bristol Channel. There was no way of getting into Barry. The berths in Cardiff were taken, so it was up the river to Bristol, the only port of refuge available. As the season only had a couple of days to go, it was decided to finish sailings for the summer then. Under the circumstances, this wasn't an unpopular decision, and the crew were paid off for that year.

1954 was a year of firsts for *Cardiff Queen*. On a personal note, it was the first time I had been in charge of the ship. It was also the first visit of a paddle steamer to Lynmouth after the disastrous floods in 1952; the first visit of one of the ships to Bideford for 30 years; the first Campbell's steamer to call at Tenby since before the War.

Cardiff Queen backing away from Ilfracombe.

We sailed from Bristol on 2nd June for Ilfracombe, calling at Clevedon, Cardiff, Penarth and Barry. With about 500 passengers aboard the ship sailed from Ilfracombe for Lynmouth. Under the circumstances it was a very touching occasion, felt by all of us who had previously known the place and the people. It was a good day for us; a great day for them.

Our usual calls to embark and disembark passengers by launch there were carried out 'on the run'. Coming down-Channel, the boats would be waiting inside Foreland Point, we would keep steerage way on the ship, and the passengers were put on board and taken off underway. Coming up-Channel, we carried out the reverse operation from Highveer Point. This was only safe and practicable because of the knowledge and experience of Tom Richards and his boatmen colleagues. The number of passengers handled at any one time seldom exceeded the capacity of a couple of boats. But on this day, we had several hundred passengers to go ashore, and of course the local civic dignitaries to bring on board for a formal reception. These kind of arrangements don't always go according to plan. This almost did.

We dropped anchor as near as possible to the landing stage. The contest between the wind and tide for supremacy didn't afford a very good lee for the boats, so inevitably there was some uncomfortable movement for those getting off and on. Mr. Banks the joint M.D. came on the bridge and asked me to stop landing passengers as it was unsafe. For official reasons he was supposed to go ashore at Lynmouth, but didn't fancy the idea. Smith-Cox, who was present at the time, indicated diplomatically that as Mr. Banks was a passenger on the ship he had the same right of refusal as the other 499, and didn't need to get off if he didn't wish to. A delicate matter was thus resolved.

Two days later, *Cardiff Queen* made her historic visit to Bideford. There was an unforgettable civic reception on Bideford quay when it seemed the whole town had turned out to welcome the ship. We berthed starboard side to the Quay expecting to have a good bit of ebb tide to swing the ship round on leaving. The River Torridge was in no way as lively as the Avon or the Usk, or even the Tawe, and swinging the ship with ropes to head downstream proved quite a struggle. As always we made it, but not as quickly as we would have liked. Members of the

Cardiff Queen 1954. Civic welcome at Bideford Quay to commemorate first visit for thirty years.

North Devon Council boarded and joined the ship over to Swansea for a reception by the Mayor and City Council on arrival. It was my first visit to the Guildhall in Swansea. After lunch there, Mayor T.S. (Tommy) Harris insisted that 'the Captain say a few words'. It was the first time I had spoken in public. It was inconceivable then that some forty years later I would be doing it quite regularly as a member of Swansea City Council. Councillor Harris and other members joined the North Devon party for the return trip to Ilfracombe and Bideford. Crowds crammed every vantage-point to see the ship arrive. The weather wasn't quite so good on the return to Swansea in the early hours of the morning. It was quite a day.

The first visit to Tenby by a paddle steamer since before the war took place in July 1954. Tenby Pier, like Minehead, had been demolished for defence reasons, and was never rebuilt. Now it may seem quite

Cardiff Queen leaving Tenby on her first trip in 1954.

unnecessary to have gone to the trouble to knock down piers in case of a German invasion. Those who remember events after Dunkirk may have different views.

Berthing a ship the size of *Cardiff Queen* at Tenby presented some problems. The seaward end of the pier wasn't considered suitable, so we decided to use the inside of the breakwater. Small boats were told by the Council to keep well clear of the berth. All but one did. The starboard paddle wheel picked up its moorings. We were later told the boat was owned by the official who issued the keep-clear notice. No damage ensued.

Most Tenby trips were very successful. One of the schedules tried was Swansea, Tenby, Lundy, Ilfracombe, Lundy, Tenby, Swansea. Landing passengers at Lundy, leaving them there, and returning several hours later to pick them up was considered too risky weatherwise and

was stopped. A cruise from Ilfracombe along the North Devon coast to off Lynmouth was substituted. The weather always seemed to be fine when we visited Tenby, and with few exceptions there were large crowds of passengers waiting to board. Subsequently, the seaward end of the breakwater was fitted with vertical wooden piling. This made berthing easier, particularly at night.

The first visit of the Royal Yacht *Britannia* to the Bristol Channel was in August 1955. This provided a great opportunity for another first by *Cardiff Queen*. *Britannia* anchored in Milford Haven. We sailed from Swansea to Ilfracombe and then to Milford, tying up at the entrance to Milford Dock to embark passengers for a cruise around the Royal Yacht further down the Haven.

Turning a paddle-steamer in a limited space is its major difficulty. *Britannia* was lying at anchor to the ebb tide. Our passengers had a

Cardiff Queen at Milford Haven, dressed overall for the visit of Her Majesty's Yacht Britannia.

this didn't show the Naval defence boom across the entrance. The ship was at the point of no return when the boom was spotted. We picked our way slowly between two of the buoys. When the pilot eventually came on board I said we had come over the chains of the boom and not through the centre channel. 'You're in good company,' he said. 'So did *Britannia*, he didn't have a pilot on board either.'

A bonus for the Swansea and Ilfracombe passengers was another good view. The Royal children, Charles and Anne (then aged six and four) were playing in a cove on the port side of the Haven as we entered.

BRITANNIA. Built by S. McKnight & Co, Ayr, 1896. Length 230 ft. Beam 26 ft. Speed 19 knots.

Built at Ayr on the Firth of Clyde in 1896, *Britannia* was arguably the fastest of all White Funnel paddle steamers. There will always be controversy when the relative speeds of ships are discussed, particularly in the Bristol Channel where the use of tide to advantage considerably influences time on a run. Speed over the initial measured mile on trials is not always a reliable guide to future operational performances. Important factors are inevitably the person in charge on the bridge, the person on the wheel, and those working the engines.

Britannia had the reputation of being mollycoddled, as Captain Peter Campbell's 'baby'. Older colleagues who were in the company for many years told me stories of him going on board the ship before sailing, putting on a pair of white gloves and running his hands along deck and engine-room beams checking for cleanliness.

In 1953 *Glen Gower*, *Bristol Queen*, and *Cardiff Queen* went south for the Coronation Review, leaving *Britannia*, *Ravenswood* and *Glen Usk* to hold the fort in the Bristol Channel. I was appointed to take *Britannia* to Swansea. Bill Watson asked if I would have him as chief officer as he didn't want to go with Captain Archie Harris, and that was one way out of it. However, the best laid plans . . . don't always work. Archie, on return from the Review, was asked which ship he wanted to

great view of *Britannia*'s bow. Those on *Britannia* had a very close view of *Cardiff Queen*. By their actions, some seemed to feel it was too close, including the pilot. He looked relieved when the engines were put full ahead and *Cardiff Queen* responded well.

Never having been in Milford with a ship before, I depended on picking up the pilot we had ordered outside. There was no sign of a pilot-boat when we approached. We proceeded in, using the chart, but

Britannia's maiden trip. There was always enough water for *Britannia*, the best paddle steamer of them all for steering and handling.

Britannia leaving Swansea, July 27 1953: master, George Gunn; mate, Bill Watson. There was a very rough sea and swell, the wind WNW F7. The Ilfracombe to Lundy trip was subsequently cancelled.

take over as master, chose *Britannia*, and relieved me on her at Swansea. The old adversaries teamed up again and sailed *Britannia* until the end of that season.

Britannia was—for a paddle-steamer—a wonderful ship to handle, but she wasn't popular on the Swansea run, having replaced *Cardiff Queen* which by then was well-liked. People who criticised *Cardiff Queen*'s motion in a seaway had never sailed on *Britannia* from Swansea to Ilfracombe in bad weather! She was used to much more sedate passages than can be experienced at that end of the Channel. To compensate for this, in fine weather *Britannia* made faster passages than anything her predecessors had done, and was easier and quicker to berth and swing in the confines of the River Tawe at Swansea. Having by then been master of *Ravenswood* and *Glen Gower* I would have given *Britannia* 8 out of 10. I liked her, but she was not ideal for Swansea. Based at Bristol or Cardiff, heading down- and up-Channel, *Britannia* definitely scored 10 out of 10!

Although *Bristol Queen* assumed the title of Flagship of the Fleet, this was never really accepted by the older fraternity. As far as they were concerned it was still *Britannia*, and the esteem in which this exceptional ship was held remained throughout her years with the company.

Some Bristol-Channel legends had been in charge of this ship during her career—Captain Peter Campbell himself, Dan Taylor then Jack George before the War. Being given the opportunity in 1953 was quite a thrill for me, and a challenge, as her chief engineer at that time was Tom Price who had sailed in the Old Guv'nor's days, and kept us informed on the way he, and the others, had successfully made *Britannia* 'the best paddle-steamer anywhere'. As purser Jim Keating said to me when I was appointed to *Britannia*: 'That ship's like a greyhound, "something" and ribs, built for speed, nothing else'.

Captain Bert Murphy was the last sailing master of *Britannia*. Bert had been with the Company before the War as mate, transferred to the Royal Navy with the ships, and was master of *Glen Gower* after she went back into service for Campbells. When it was decided to lay up *Britannia*, Bert received a letter in the mail informing him that his employment was terminated. Being a P.& A. man through and through, and by then quite senior in company service, his departure in that manner was very difficult to swallow.

Mementoes from Campbells' ships are widely distributed, and much sought after. My most prized ones are mounted on the wall of my office at home: *Britannia*'s clock and barometer. Like all else connected to this unique vessel, they were ultra-efficient, and now— at over 100 years old—the barometer forecasts weather-changes with unerring accuracy.

SISTERLY RIVALRY

There was always controversy about the respective merits of the two newest Campbell ships *Bristol Queen* and *Cardiff Queen*. The general opinion seems to have been that *Bristol Queen* was the better of the two vessels. Having sailed both ships on so many occasions, I would not agree with that entirely. Each had its own good points and not so good ones, although a combination of the best features of both would no doubt result in a near perfect paddle steamer.

Throughout the 1950s *Cardiff Queen* was almost continuously on the Swansea station, acknowledged as the bad weather run. I look at my old bridge movement-books now and note that the weather conditions 'Fresh/Strong Westerly Winds, Heavy Sea & Swell' occur very frequently during those years. Opening up the Channel after Mumbles Head with a Force 6 or 7 on the starboard beam could be quite upsetting to many passengers, and often crew-members. Wind strengths in excess of that were good reasons to stay in port.

Having made well over 1000 cross-Channel passages with *Cardiff Queen*, I admit there were a number of anxious moments. Unlike propellers, paddles are very exposed to the impact of heavy seas. The shallow draft and light construction of the ship itself make careful handling in a seaway, and bringing a paddle-steamer carefully alongside, absolute priorities.

Apart from minor damages, *Cardiff Queen*'s record of performance on very rough passages was quite remarkable and trouble-free. *Bristol Queen*'s life during these years was very different. She was mainly employed on good weather runs: Bristol or Cardiff to Ilfracombe. Similar wind-conditions existed, but they had comparatively little effect on the ship or her performance. She operated up and down the Channel with the prevailing winds ahead or astern, and the benefit of the shelter of the land. It is amazing how *Cardiff Queen* stood up to what she was asked to do so successfully.

In terms of speed, most people think that *Bristol Queen* was much the faster of the two. The fact that her fastest time—with the tide—for the 21 nautical miles from Lundy to Ilfracombe was 59 minutes as against *Cardiff Queen*'s best of 61 minutes, suggests that there was not that much in it, although *Cardiff Queen* did slow down more in bad weather.

Bridge Comparisons. *Cardiff Queen* berthed at Ilfracombe with *Bristol Queen* moored outside her.

Mumbles Pier

The re-opening of Mumbles Pier in 1956 greatly improved Swansea and Porthcawl sailing schedules. Until then the tidal limits at the berths in the River Tawe severely restricted passenger services. The availability of the Pier at all states of tide changed that.

By then, *Cardiff Queen* was firmly established as the Swansea Boat and was very popular with passengers. This was rather different to when she replaced *Glen Gower* at Swansea in 1950. At the time, there was still contention between Cardiff and Swansea about their relative importance to the Principality. Although Cardiff is now the capital city, even now rivalry still prevails. Campbell's were considered thoughtless in sending a ship named *Cardiff Queen* to replace a ship named *Glen Gower* at Swansea, at this crucial time. It says something for *Cardiff Queen* that long before 1956 her popularity had been firmly established.

Since she sailed daily from Swansea, it was assumed that *Cardiff Queen* would perform the opening ceremony at Mumbles, and be the first ship into the Pier. That was not to be; the Company decided we changed over with *Bristol Queen* at Ilfracombe the day before the event. Captain George and his ship opened the Pier, and *Cardiff Queen* took up the Bristol run for a couple of days before changing back again to Swansea. The very nice presentation by Mumbles Chamber of Trade inscribed 'To Capt. G. Gunn, To Mark the Re-Opening of Mumbles Pier, 9th June, 1956,' was passed on to me by Jack George. It is good news to hear that now, forty years on, there are moves to raise finance to put the Pier and Landing Stage back into full operation. Let's hope they are successful. It is something Waverley Excursions who operate P.S. *Waverley* and M.V. *Balmoral* have wanted for many years, in order to provide better passenger services to the area. I may have just missed the first re-opening, but hope to be at the next one!

The Grounding that wasn't

My first season as Master of *Cardiff Queen* on the Swansea run was 1954. The weather was generally poor, with strong westerly winds, rough seas and plenty of rain, especially in July.

Bank Holiday Monday 2nd August should have been the busiest day of the summer, with two return-trips between Swansea and Ilfracombe and a Gower-Coast cruise. The following extract from the bridge movement-book should clarify events, and show that the ship never grounded in the River Tawe.

Cardiff Queen departed Swansea 9.12am, arrived Ilfracombe 11.10 and left there at 11.20. Arrived South Dock Jetty 1.26pm after embarking a large number of passengers for the cruise. It was late on tide, and for the second and last time in the years with Campbells I went against my better judgement and sailed when the ship should have stayed there and the cruise cancelled. The factors which I remember prompted that decision were: a reluctance to disappoint so many people on their Bank Holiday, and trade so far that season had been bad because of the weather.

There was nothing to spare at that state of the tide with a ship 250 feet long swinging round in the river. Once around, heading downstream in the middle, there was sufficient water to get out, taking it easy on the engines. We didn't quite get to that point of the operation as the following log book entry shows:

After swinging at 1.36 let go the cant rope, ship proceeded down river, but owing to strong freshet (result of continuous heavy rain upriver from Swansea) and a strong ebb tide on the port quarter, she took a sheer across the river, ending beam on by the force of it, and as the ship's stern swung round, touched an underwater obstruction inside the breakwater.

Let go starboard anchor 1.42 pm and with this just on the bottom the ship was dredged stern first down the river and out into the buoyed channel. At 2.35 heave up anchor between buoys and proceed stern first towards Mumbles. At 2.55 let go starboard anchor. Steering gear inspected and all working parts found to be in order. 3.10 pm heave up anchor and proceed on cruise. 3.15 vessel carrying an unusual amount of starboard helm. 4.10pm turned off Port Eynon Point. Message morsed to Mumbles Coastguard Station at 4.40 pm, 'Will you please ask agent to arrange for ship repair representative to meet us on arrival at Swansea, as I think we have a damaged rudder.' G. Gunn, Master.

5.00pm. Mumbles abeam. 5.12 Outer Fairway Buoy. 5.24 vessel unable to steer in approach channel, let go starboard anchor. Message sent to pilot cutter Roger Beck for their assistance to berth in Swansea. 6.30pm anchor aweigh, passed rope from bow to Roger Beck. 7.10 pm arrive Pockets Wharf. 7.30 pm moored and finished with engines.

Examination showed the rudder-post was severely bent. The ship went to drydock in Cardiff under her own steam with one tug in attendance. This tug wasn't required to make fast to *Cardiff Queen* during the passage, but two tugs were used to assist in drydocking. After observation in drydock, it was difficult to believe the ship could have steamed the distances she did unaided.

There was a lighter side to the incident. On that day Glamorgan were playing the West Indies at St.Helen's cricket-ground which overlooks Swansea Bay. The late Brian Johnston was doing a radio commentary. In between overs he said, 'There's a ship out in the Bay with two white funnels; it's going around in circles and it seems to be in trouble'. Captain Slater, the Swansea Dockmaster, was sitting at home enjoying the cricket. He jumped into his car, drove down to the Kings Dock Jetty and sent Roger Beck out to see what was wrong.

Some time later, *Cardiff Queen* was taking part in one of BBC's live 'Saturday Night Out' television broadcasts at Weston Pier with Brian Johnston and Raymond Baxter. I asked Brian whether he remembered the incident. 'Very well,' he said, but added, 'Those West Indies are not really very good cricketers.' What a difference forty years can make!

Glamorgan won what I understand was a good match, and a memorable victory. Because perhaps it never had the significance of some other notable events, the question, 'Where were you on the day Glamorgan beat the West Indies?' has never been asked, nor has the answer, 'Going round in circles in Swansea Bay on *Cardiff Queen*' ever been given in answer. I would like to hear from anyone else who could give that answer.

The answer to another question, 'When is a grounding not a grounding?' is: 'when the rudder strikes an unidentified underwater object.'

Little Sister's Big Day

Sunday 19th August 1956 opened cloudy and clear with a moderate to fresh south-westerly wind, moderate sea and swell; a good sailing day. *Cardiff Queen* left Swansea at 10.00am, Mumbles Pier 10.25 and arrived at Ilfracombe 12.10pm. We left the Pier at 1.30pm and stood off awaiting *Bristol Queen* to berth and embark passengers for Tenby. She sailed at 2.16pm. At 2.30pm we received a message from *Bristol Queen* to make for her position as she was stopped with paddle-wheel problems. Towing one paddle steamer with another in strong tides and with a bit of wind on the beam was another experience as both ships were only drawing about seven feet of water, and the drag of *Bristol Queen*'s paddle-floats didn't help. It needed 3 x 120 fathoms of mooring rope (about 2,000 feet) to get any steering control of *Cardiff Queen*. I was sure Captain George on *Bristol Queen* had his helmsman valiantly, but rather fruitlessly under these circumstances, turning the steering wheel in a token gesture to relieve the ignominy of the situation which had befallen the flagship of the fleet.

My feelings, as I remember them were very different, and quite confident despite the towage difficulties: we would get *Bristol Queen* and her passengers to a safe anchorage . . . sometime. Should *Cardiff Queen* not have been available, there was the possibility of a large salvage claim. This would have been assessed not only on the value of the ship, but the cargo carried, in this case the passengers.

At 7.35pm we both anchored in Mumbles Roads. *Cardiff Queen* went alongside the Pier at 8.07 and left there at 8.15 taking all the passengers back home to Ilfracombe, after a different kind of day trip from what they had expected. We arrived in Ilfracombe at 9.57 and were back at Mumbles Pier by midnight.

The ship's Log records the weather as *Light/Moderate SW Wind, Slight Sea & Swell, Fine & Clear. Towing Distance = 21 Miles. Time = 4.00 Hrs. Av.Spd. = 5.25 Kts.*

For services rendered the insurance underwriters authorised a sum of £2OO to be apportioned between the members of the crew. I received an *ex-gratia* payment of £20.

WHITE FUNNEL PURSERS

A qualification for purser in Campbells was a First or Second Class Radio Certificate. Others included the ability to handle most of the Company's cash flow, attend gangways at all times, spot passengers who had forgotten to pay the fare, make every public address announcement, and man the front line of defence—the ticket office window. Apart from this, and attending to, and answering, all correspondence, writing up the official log-books, and encouraging the master, mate and chief engineer to sign them promptly, balancing the books, and banking the days' spoils, there was little else to do . . .

All Campbells' pursers were former radio officers in the Merchant Navy. They gave up the best job at sea for home comforts and more work.

SYD PARTINGTON married into the prolific Tyrell family, which featured prominently in the success of the catering departments on P.& A. ships before and after the War. Syd was purser of *Empress Queen* and my landlord for my first five years in the Company. He owned a block of flats in Horfield, Bristol. These were preferentially rented to selected Campbell's employees. John Whiten, purser of *Ravenswood*, myself and our families occupied two of them. Even in 1948 the inclusive rental of one pound a week, which Syd occasionally collected on a Saturday, was good value for money. That the building was directly opposite the main entrance to Horfield Prison didn't matter. Jim

Syd Parkington, purser of *Empress Queen.*

Keating, purser of *Glen Usk,* with his usual Irish wit named it 'Casa Campbell'. Why not? Syd was also the company's shore electrician during the winter lay-up period. Whatever latent talent was unearthed in an officer was evaluated and put to use accordingly in the winter.

BILL FORBES was on *Glen Gower* and *Cardiff Queen* on the Swansea run with Captain Bert Murphy when I first met him. Bill could have been considered abrupt by those who didn't know him. Unfortunately, this included most passengers. I liked him.

BILL BERRY was our purser on *Cardiff Queen* at Swansea in the 1950s. We became good friends. Bill was a bit pedantic with some passengers, and 'adjustments to the course' were occasionally made. On one passage from Ilfracombe to Swansea we were about to pass ahead of a large sailing vessel on its way up-Channel. I blew down the voicepipe to Bill and said, 'Tell the passengers that on the port side they can see the Italian Naval Training Vessel *Amerigo Vespucci*.' 'Alright, alright', he replied. Immediately the announcement came through the loudspeakers, 'Ladies and gentlemen, on the port side you can see the Italian Naval Training ship . . . what's the bloody thing's name?' I guessed he hadn't got it first time.

JIM KEATING had been a ship's wireless operator in the 1920s and 1930s. He sailed out of Cardiff on the tough old tramps before joining Campbells. In those days wireless operators were looked at as superfluous to requirements by shipowners and masters, mates and engineers who sailed their ships. Sparks, as they were known, received no favours, and supplied all their own necessities for the voyage themselves. His ship was loading coal in Cardiff. When buying his sea-stores at the shop near the dock entrance, Jim was asked by the salesman, as was usual, what ship he was on, and where bound and when were they sailing. Jim told him that they were just finishing cargo and sailing that evening. For some reason the ship was delayed and didn't go.

Jim decided to do some dhobeying (washing clothes). His purchases included toothpaste, toilet soap and some cartons of Sunlight washing soap. These were packed in long cardboard boxes, two tablets to each. When he opened a box, one compartment had a bar of soap and the other one was stuffed with brown paper. They were all the same. The cargo of coal Jim's ship was loading must have been for a long trip to the River Plate and not a short trip to the Mediterranean. The ship chandler knew that!

Jim Keating's Irish wit, worldly experience, thoughtfulness, and popularity with passengers made him an ace of pursers. Every ship needed a Jim Keating, but they weren't always available.

JOHN WHITEN was purser on *Ravenswood* for three years. He came from Grimsby, and was a fish connoisseur. John left Campbells to take over a pub at Dowlais Top, South Wales. He certainly learned the basics there, before going back home to take over as steward of Cleethorpes Golf Club.

CHARLIE WALL was a former radio officer with Blue Funnel Line. The efficiency of 'Blue Flu' certainly rubbed off on Charles. Everything he did in his job as a purser and in the Underfall Yard in the winter was according to the book. He was a great family man, and was married to Fay, a member of one of the world-renowned Pill Pilot families. Charlie Wall became very much associated with *Bristol Queen* in her latter years.

EDDIE WOODS was the youngest of the post-War Campbell pursers. He was very jovial, enjoyed life and working with Captain Archie Harris our Marine Superintendent.

BILL BANKS JNR. was the son of the managing director. He was an assistant purser on *Empress Queen* with Syd Partington. He was a very pleasant young man who really enjoyed the Torquay to Channel Islands service the ship was on for one year. The real bonus was that he met his beautiful wife there, who was a receptionist in the Imperial Hotel in Torquay.

Dear old Charles (Wall) on this occasion did not smile. Fred Birmingham has a doubtful 'tweak' about it all.

WHITE FUNNEL ENGINEERS

SPENCER SOLOMAN was chief engineer of *Glen Gower* when I was there in 1950 and 1951, relieving Joe Phillips. Spencer was a pre-War stalwart who was commissioned into the RNR with the ships at the outbreak of war. He was a large man with an unfortunate speech impediment. On an early occasion, leaving Penarth Pier on the way into Cardiff, I put the engine telegraph on half speed at the Outer Wrack Buoy. The ship's speed was reduced accordingly. Further in towards the berth we appeared to be gradually slowing down without any bridge telegraph movements. I investigated this on arrival at the pontoon and discovered the second engineer had been positioned at the paddle-box door, informing Spencer Soloman at the engine-controls of the ship's progress towards the berth. He was shutting in the speed of the engine without instructions from the bridge. This didn't happen again; Spencer and I got on quite well afterwards.

SYD LEONARD was chief engineer of *Britannia* and *Cardiff Queen*. A Cornishman from Mevagissey, he was not always happy on the Swansea run. He felt I pushed the ship a bit in bad weather. He was a very clever engineer, and his hobby was building model steam-locomotives. He left Campbells to work as plant-engineer with Showerings of Taunton.

RON HILLIER was chief engineer of *Empress Queen*. He knew the ship inside-out. He had a dispute with the Company about a salary increase. There was no agreement, so Ron left. The ship subsequently went to Avonmouth for a pre-season drydocking with Captain Kidd in charge. Leaving there she came astern into the quay a couple of times when the engines should have been going ahead, causing damage and delay. We understood at the time that the financial inducement to Hillier's successor to take over as chief engineer of *Empress Queen*

would have been sufficient to have kept Ron in the job he knew so well, and had that been the case the engines would have corresponded to the telegraph movements.

JACK GILES was chief engineer of *Bristol Queen*. He was a good, experienced paddle steamer engineer. To be in charge of *B.Q.* he had to be the best. When Captain Jack George went ahead or astern on the engine telegraphs it had to happen immediately, and it did. Running with the tide at Clevedon or Penarth (and there was no turning round to stem the tide), needed perfect cohesion between bridge and engine-room. The two Jacks had it, so did *Bristol Queen*. *Cardiff Queen* and *Britannia* managed to run with the tide at piers, but never *Ravenswood*, *Glen Usk* or *Glen Gower*. Unless of course the tidal strength was minimal; then we would show off.

JOHNNY TAYLOR was chief engineer of *Glen Usk* and son of Captain Dan Taylor, the pre-War marine superintendent of the Company, and a well-known master of *Britannia* in her heyday. The combined P.& A. service of Johnny, Captain Findley Brander, the mate Dave Miles and purser Jim Keating on *Glen Usk* was hard to beat. So was the manner and efficiency of their operation of *Glen Usk* on the Cardiff/Weston ferry. None of them wanted to go anywhere else and made sure they didn't have to.

TOM PRICE was chief engineer of *Britannia*. Another old pre-War company man, he was a good raconteur of 'What it used to be like in the old Guv'nor's time'. He was easy to work with and didn't bother me as master with engine problems. He sorted everything 'below' out himself. What more can a ship's captain expect from an engineer?

ALEX CAMPBELL was chief engineer of *Ravenswood* and later *Cardiff Queen*. He was a son of Captain Peter Campbell. Alex died in the engine-room of *Cardiff Queen* alongside Ilfracombe on Sunday 13th September, 1959. There's much to remember about Alex. One trivial thing was his love for Worcester sauce. 'Steward, where's the Lea & Perrins?' always rang out if there wasn't a bottle on the table. Whatever the dish, it was always more than adequately coated.

Alex Campell always looked on the brighter side of life.

EASTER SAILINGS

Every year, one of the ships came out at Easter to start up the Cardiff to Weston ferry service. Being the first holiday break after the winter, Easter weekend (weather permitting) was good business from Cardiff. Why shouldn't it also be good for Swansea to Ilfracombe? The ships by now were laid up for the winter in Penarth Dock, and we could easily get *Cardiff Queen* ready for a limited operation from Good Friday through to Tuesday. Finish then, and back to Penarth until Whitsun.

Clifton Smith-Cox, our managing director, took some convincing. No Campbell ship had ever run from Swansea to Ilfracombe as early as Easter. Not being a strict traditionalist, however, he agreed to try it out.

The ship was made presentable, and with a scratch crew sailed from Cardiff to Swansea at 9.50am on Good Friday and made her first trip from there at 2.30pm over to Ilfracombe after calling at Mumbles. The weather was not very promising. It was cold, and it snowed. On Saturday we were scheduled to do two trips between Swansea and Ilfracombe and an afternoon cruise along the Gower Coast. It blew and rained. By the time we were on our way back in the evening, it was getting a bit depressing. I was beginning to wish I had kept quiet about Easter sailings from Swansea. Still, there were Sunday and Monday to come, and they were the important days for passenger traffic. The weather was bound to improve, the barometer was rising, and with it my hopes for a better day ahead. We had to get a break on Sunday, if not, it didn't matter what happened on Easter Monday, the whole idea would be a washout in every way.

Strong winds, snow and heavy rain are not the best ingredients for pleasure cruising. It is significant that the newspaper report of the excursion, 'Season's First Trip', appears next to a headline: 'W. Wales has snow during "Arctic Easter". No better prospects, say weather forecasters.' By Monday all possibility of a viable financial weekend had gone, as did any chance of Easter sailings in future years from Swansea to Ilfracombe. Smith-Cox sportingly said 'It *was* your idea George, not mine, although I had thought of trying it out.'

EASTER HOLIDAYS 1958

Sailings from
SWANSEA AND MUMBLES
SOUTH DOCK ENTRANCE, SWANSEA AND MUMBLES PIER

GOOD FRIDAY, APRIL 4th

Afternoon Trip to ILFRACOMBE. Leave Swansea 2.30 p.m., Mumbles 2.50 p.m. Leave Ilfracombe 7.15 p.m. for Mumbles and Swansea. Special cheap return fare 15/6d.
Note : A steamer leaves Cardiff 9.50 a.m. for Swansea.

SATURDAY, APRIL 5th

Day trip to ILFRACOMBE. Leave Swansea 9.45 a.m., Mumbles 10.5 a.m. Leave Ilfracombe 12.30 or 7.45 p.m. for Mumbles and Swansea.
Combined Steamer and Coach Tour to WESTWARD HO and BIDEFORD. An attractive Afternoon Tour via Braunton, Barnstaple, Instow, Bideford and Northam to the Golden Sands and famous pebble ridge at Westward Ho. Leave Swansea 9.45 a.m., Mumbles 10.5 a.m. Leave Ilfracombe 7.45 p.m. for Mumbles and Swansea. Inclusive Return Fare 25/-. Children 14/6d. Coach leaves Ilfracombe (Pier Gates) at 2.15 p.m.
Afternoon Cruise along the GOWER COAST. Leave Mumbles 2.45 p.m., Swansea 3.15 p.m.; back Swansea 5.15 p.m., Mumbles 5.30 p.m. Fare 6/6d.
Evening trip to ILFRACOMBE. Leave Swansea 5.30 p.m., Mumbles 5.50 p.m. Leave Ilfracombe 7.45 p.m. for Mumbles and Swansea. Fare (single or return; this trip only) 10/6d.
Note : Steamer leaves Ilfracombe 12.30 p.m. for Mumbles and Swansea.

EASTER SUNDAY, APRIL 6th

Day trip to PORTHCAWL. Leave Swansea 8.0 a.m. Leave Porthcawl 8.50 p.m. for Mumbles and Swansea.
Day trip to ILFRACOMBE and afternoon Cruise off LYNMOUTH. Leave Swansea 10.45 a.m., Mumbles 11.5 a.m. Leave Ilfracombe 5.15 p.m. for Mumbles and Swansea. (Steamer leaves Ilfracombe for Cruise at 3.0 p.m.)
Evening Cruise calling at PORTHCAWL. Leave Mumbles 7.0 p.m., Swansea 7.30 p.m.; back Mumbles 9.50 p.m., Swansea 10.10 p.m. Fare 5/-.

EASTER MONDAY, APRIL 7th

Day trip to ILFRACOMBE and LUNDY ISLAND (to land) or afternoon Cruise to BIDEFORD BAY. Leave Swansea 9.45 a.m., Mumbles 10.5 a.m., Lundy Island 4.45 p.m. Leave Ilfracombe 6.30 p.m. for Mumbles and Swansea. (Passengers for Cruise change steamers at Ilfracombe in each direction and leave at 2.30 p.m.)
Combined steamer and coach tour via ILFRACOMBE to HUNTERS INN, by way of Two Potts and Berrydown, allowing two hours to view the Inn and walk to Heddons-mouth, returning via Trentishoe Common and Combe Martin. Leave Swansea 9.45 a.m., Mumbles 10.5 a.m. Leave Ilfracombe 6.30 p.m. for Mumbles and Swansea. Inclusive return fare 25/-, children 14/-. Coach leaves Ilfracombe (Pier Gates) at 2.15 p.m.

TUESDAY, APRIL 8th

Day trip to ILFRACOMBE and afternoon cruise off LYNMOUTH. Leave Swansea 9.45 a.m., Mumbles 10.5 a.m. Leave Ilfracombe 4.45 p.m. for Mumbles and Swansea. (Steamer leaves Ilfracombe for Cruise 2.30 p.m.)
Single trip to PENARTH PIER (for Cardiff). Leave Mumbles 6.25 p.m., Swansea 7.0 p.m. Fare 10/6d.

For fares and general information see overleaf

Cardiff Queen passing Outer Fairway buoy on her way into Swansea.

(photo:World Ship Society)

WHITE FUNNEL PLACES

Weston Pier (Birnbeck Island)

The most difficult berthing in the Bristol and English Channels for paddle steamers was at Weston-Super-Mare. The constantly changing direction of the tidal set near the Pier was a major cause of delays to the ships. Passengers on board, and those waiting on the Pier to embark, must sometimes have thought the officers on the bridge were 'not quite with it', because of the strange manner they adopted to try to get the ships alongside. It was never easy, but more difficult at some states of the tide than others. The rule was, take nothing for granted, as Weston will make a fool of you just when you thought it was going to be OK.

Many theories were expressed as to how it should be done; they were usually put forward by those who'd never had to do it, or with little experience of handling White Funnel paddle steamers. I was one of the theorists and made it known after only a few weeks on *Ravenswood*,

using the Pier every day, at every state of the tide, that a graph could be compiled to know what to expect.

I mentioned this to Bob Campbell, the Company's Weston agent and son of the founder. Bob's face went even redder than usual; he had heard that kind of thing from others, and they had all come to grief. 'It just doesn't work at Weston. This place is different from anywhere else the ships call at, or ever have done, so don't waste your time laddie!' He was right. It didn't work. The main lessons to be learnt at Weston were not to be over-confident, and to know when to get out of it and have another go.

One fine Sunday morning in 1950, four ships were due out of Weston within a short time of each other. Captains Bill Watson *(Ravenswood)* and Brander *(Glen Usk)* from Cardiff; George Gunn *(Glen Gower)* from Newport; and Jack George *(Bristol Queen)* from Bristol. Good sailing weather with a big spring tide.

Close work off Weston for *Britannia*, *Glen Usk* and *Glen Avon*. Two of three survived the war: *Glen Avon* foundered off the French coast in 1940.

The first ship to go in was *Glen Usk*. She corkscrewed around and Brander had to back out. The *Ravenswood*'s flag went up on the Pier, Watson had a go and missed. *Glen Gower* was then called in; this was my chance to show them how to do it; almost, but not quite—I suffered the same fate as the others. Weston was at its benign-looking worst. It was one-and-a-half hours to flow (an hour and a half before high water at Bristol). The time when the swill at the approach end of the Pier constantly changed and caused the trouble. The Pier foreman stood at the corner throwing rolled-up pieces of paper into the water to show him the direction of the tidal set, and indicated this to the approaching ship by waving what looked like a very large white table-tennis bat. *Glen Usk*, *Ravenswood* and *Glen Gower*, having missed at their first attempt, were reforming to have another go when *Bristol Queen* appeared around Sand Point going hell for leather. Captain Jack George was unaware of what had happened, and must have been surprised to see the other three ships still there. Brander on *Glen Usk* was over-ready for another go, and although *Bristol Queen*'s flag was hoisted, made for the pier against the signal. The thought of Jack George—his avowed rival—beating him in under these circumstances was unacceptable. Brander did get a rope up, but *Glen Usk* was carried around inside the pier, putting the ship in a very dangerous position. Should it have parted she would have been swept down under the bridge with dreadful consequences. After much pulling and hauling, *Glen Usk* made it and was eventually moored at the face of the pier. When she left we all took our turn to berth. By then the tide was more sympathetic, and the fun was over. So was the possibility of punctual day's sailings for *Bristol Queen* and *Ravenswood*. *Bristol Queen* carried on down to Ilfracombe, *Glen Usk* made another trip on the Ferry. *Ravenswood* lost a trip and retired to Cardiff for the rest of the tide. *Glen Gower* went to Barry and sat it out until the afternoon cruise.

Ravenswood's problems didn't end at Weston. Captain Watson decided there was still enough water to go through the 'gut' in the Cardiff Sands. On entering this spot someone noticed a coil of five-inch rope running out over the side through a stern fairlead. He shouted up to the bridge, but Bill wouldn't stop the ship there on the ebb tide. One hundred and twenty fathoms of new mooring rope disappeared astern. It was never seen or heard of again.

Weston-Super-Mare was the focal point of all passenger steamer operations in the upper reaches of the Bristol Channel for many years. Every Campbell steamer except *Empress Queen* did spells on the Cardiff to Weston ferry. Like today's Dover to Calais operations, quick berthing and efficient handling of passengers was necessary to maintain the tight sailing schedules and the interchange of passengers between ships. The photograph overleaf of *Ravenswood* is a particularly interesting one. The state of tide has to be about one hour before High Water. Jack George used to do this sometimes with *Bristol Queen*. I have done it with *Cardiff Queen* and *Britannia*, but not with any of the 'low powered' ships such as *Ravenswood*, *Glen Gower* or *Glen Usk*. They often ended up port side to the pier . . . unintentionally, at 'an hour and a half to flow'.

No paddle steamer would of course, try this after high water whatever the height of tide, as it isn't possible to bring a paddle steamer in at the correct angle to land on the strongest part of the sponson, the after-knuckle. And, of course, a strong ebb setting down through the pier would be disastrous to a ship 'caught out' in the wrong position. Coming in from the other direction there was always the chance to back out and try again, which very often happened at Weston.

In the 1950s Captain Jack Wide ran the pier. He was a former master in Campbells and was a director of the Weston Pier Company. The number of passengers handled at Weston far exceeded any other resort at which the ships called. It was often necessary to use five gangways at a time, and the co-operation in this respect between the pier staff and ships' crews was generally excellent. Jack Wide saw to that. At awkward states of tide and bad weather, the heaving line he threw on board from the pier was often the one which saved the day. His contribution to quick turnarounds at Weston was invaluable.

Much of the passenger organising was the responsibility of Bob Campbell, the Weston agent, and elder son of the founder of the Company. He and his younger brother Alex—the chief engineer—were not unlike each other in looks, but were completely different in all other ways. It wasn't always easy with a succession of ships calling, landing passengers and embarking them for Cardiff, Bristol and Newport, often in quick rotation. Interchanging between ships almost always worked.

Ravenswood approaching Weston pier in the 1890s.

An exception was a day-trip with *Ravenswood* from Newport to Weston with a good load of passengers. After leaving the Pier in the evening for the return, the purser whistled up to the bridge on the voicepipe saying, 'Captain, I don't recognise any of these passengers!' *Glen Usk* then was alongside the Pier loading for Cardiff. Unknown to them they were actually loading for Newport, as Bob Campbell had put the Cardiff passengers on the Newport ship by mistake, and was busy directing the Newport people onto the Cardiff boat. We couldn't contact *Glen Usk* until the purser and radio officer was back in his ticket office/radio room. A message was morsed through, we both changed courses, and nobody was any the wiser . . .

Many thousands of trips were made by Campbell's steamers to Weston from 1887 until the Severn Bridge was built in 1966. The opening of the bridge was the beginning of the end of Campbells' most valuable run.

'Ferry' sailings started just before Easter and continued until late autumn. There were few people in south Wales who hadn't gone over to Weston sometime or other. Club outings on Sundays contributed considerably to the numbers carried at weekends. The fact that pubs in Wales were closed had a marked effect, and many stories have been told about the last trip on a Sunday from Weston to Cardiff. Rowdy passages were not uncommon. The master of a ship was legally the licensee of the bars, and when problems looked likely we kept them closed. The miners from the valleys, who frequently came in large numbers, took this kind of thing in good spirit and resorted to singing. In this way the hour or so on the passage was not only trouble-free, but quite enjoyable.

Things sometimes changed when we arrived at the pontoon at Cardiff, as the struggle to get off occasionally led to some differences of opinion. The Tiger Bay police who were always in attendance on these occasions, seemed to command respect from some of the more troublesome ones, especially when they addressed them by name!

Arriving at Weston too late on the tide with a full load of passengers rarely happened. When it did, there was contention regarding the cause. The traffic managers responsible for the sailings didn't allow sufficient time, or the number of passengers at Cardiff should have been restricted.

The first time it happened to me was with *Glen Gower*, with 1200 on board; the second time *Ravenswood*, with 800: both full ships. The weather was fine on both occasions. The long job of getting passengers into small boats and landing at the lifeboat slip went well. This was arranged by Jack Wide some time before we got there when he realised the ship wouldn't make it. The local boatmen were quick to respond.

Should the weather not have been favourable, it was back to Barry and a train to Cardiff. Not so easy with these numbers, and everyone's day ruined.

Because of the volume of passengers on the previous trips, *Glen Gower* was running late and it was clear at Cardiff that it would be a struggle to make the tide at Weston. Jack Guy, the Cardiff agent, felt it was unnecessary to limit the number of passengers to 500, which would have given us a fighting chance, getting away earlier from there and spending less time disembarking at Weston. 'Don't call at Penarth!' he said, but strangely kept shouting at the passengers as they came down the pontoon to embark, 'Hurry up! Time and tide wait for no man.' He was right, they didn't. Although the passengers were late, and very inconvenienced getting ashore, it was taken in good spirit. How would the media cover this today? Were people more tolerant then, and were the fairly recent years of war at that time a reason for that tolerance?

Oh, *Ravenswood*! I can't remember why we missed the tide with *Ravenswood*. It could have been something to do with steam . . .

Swansea

From the early 1920s, Campbells' steamers operated regular passenger services between Swansea and Ilfracombe. With the exception of the war years a ship was stationed throughout the season at Swansea, providing daily trips between the two ports. The Swansea boat made frequent periodic calls at Porthcawl, Minehead, Lynmouth, Tenby, Clovelly, Bideford and Lundy Island. Double trips on Saturdays and most Thursdays were a must. Saturday catered for the 'tourists' as we called them, taking a week's holiday in north Devon, and whatever the weather one trip over and back had to be made. Most passengers with luggage went over on the morning sailing. The afternoon also provided an alternative and a cruise to Ilfracombe, with a couple of hours ashore.

Thursday was early closing in Swansea, and the afternoon trip was very popular for many years.

The ships did many evening cruises from Swansea along the Gower coast and around Scarweather Light Vessel. When conditions were suitable, members of the Lightship's crew came alongside in their boat, picked up newspapers and had a quick chat with relatives and friends lining the rail on board the steamer. The crews of the lightship who worked on board for at least two weeks at a time really appreciated this, and we enjoyed doing it. In indifferent weather the ship would steam slowly to windward of the Scarweather, and the bosun, who was generally the best linesman on the paddler, would try to throw a roll of newspapers to the lightship, not always successfully. Unfortunately, they had to get there first time; there was no second chance.

The first sight I had of Swansea was when my ship anchored off Mumbles waiting for the morning tide to dock. Soon after midnight Mumbles Coastguard signalled across 'Welcome to Swansea and a Happy New Year to you all.' That was 1st January 1948. I had never heard of Campbells then.

During the 1950s and 1960s, the Port of Swansea was bursting at the seams with shipping. Frequently, every berth was occupied with vessels waiting at lay-bys, buoys, and outside in the bay at anchor. Shopkeepers in the town used to say 'When the docks are busy, so are we.' This was evident during that period.

Every merchant seaman has his own likes and dislikes of ports throughout the world. This is generally based on how far the docks are from town, and what the place and people are like when they get there. All the criteria for a good port are met in Swansea, and the popularity of the port with visiting seamen is unsurpassed anywhere.

The tanker berths in Queen's Dock are probably the closest to the town crews ever get. This may be one of the reasons so many tanker men from all over the UK married Welsh girls and settled down here. Tankers on average have less time in port than most other vessels, and are always further away from the action.

The 1950s and 1960s were boom times in the Port of Swansea. The annual shipping handled on one occasion reached a staggering twelve

Campbell's River Tawe berths at Swansea. Showing the mud at Pockett's Wharf and the south Dock Approach Jetty below the Lock entrance. Also the North Dock with a ship discharging at Weavers Mill.

Pockett's Wharf in 1997.

(Photo: Swansea City Council)

million tons. All general cargo berths were continually in use. Nine coal hoists in the Prince of Wales and Kings Dock loaded twenty-ton wagons into ships as fast as the vessels could be brought alongside, finished, taken away, and replaced with others. All main tanker jetties and coastal berths in the Queen's Dock worked to capacity, with ships at anchor outside waiting for vacancies. There were twenty-four sea pilots and fifteen harbour pilots to service the port, and as many as thirty ships had actually passed through the King's Dock Locks on one tide. The now seldom-used term 'bustling seaport' certainly applied to Swansea then.

There was plenty of coal dust everywhere in Swansea Docks during that period. Unlike today, nobody minded it, summer or winter. Harbour pilots, boatmen, berthing masters, in addition to those coaling the ships at the Prince of Wales and Kings Dock coal tips, never complained about environmental effects, or the potential health hazards of the clouds of coal dust which frequently enveloped them. Their concerns arose when there wasn't any coal dust around.

Campbells' ships seldom went into the docks; only for work to be done which was impractical at the river berths. Passengers embarked and disembarked at Pockett's Wharf, where bunker-fuel, water and stores were taken on board. The ships could only stay afloat there for about three hours either side of high water. On off-service days they remained high and dry outside of these times. Frequent shifting ship from Pockett's to the South Dock jetty took place at all odd hours during the night, to keep the ships afloat for sailing times, and to keep out of the way of ships entering and leaving the South Dock at its tide time. It was a continual game of floating musical chairs. Although a small grab dredger did its best before the season started every year to try to level the mud for the ships to lie upright, it never really succeeded. Pockett's Wharf eventually became quite unsuitable for a passenger operation, so the announcement that the British Transport Docks Board was considering building a passenger/freight terminal in the river outside the King's Dock came as good news. Could a facility for our steamers be available? After discussing the matter with them for a period of time, I received a letter of agreement setting out the cost and conditions of a move down-river. I thought it was an exceptional deal, but received some opposition.

On 25th May 1970, *Westward Ho* sailed from the new berth at the Ferryport Terminal for the first time. She and *Balmoral* were both now serviced from Swansea and between them carried out comprehensive sailing schedules throughout the Bristol Channel using the best berthing facilities to date for P. & A. ships based in the Port of Swansea.

Although now some of the facilities, such as the private adjacent car park and booking office, are no longer available, the berth at Ferryport is still being used, twenty-five years on, by *Waverley* and *Balmoral*. I understand that a rather decaying booking office structure succumbed to a series of westerly gales some years ago. A concrete plinth marks the spot.

Ilfracombe

The saying that Campbells discovered Ilfracombe is of course not true. That they have played a large part in the development of the resort as a major holiday-attraction IS true. Most places change considerably over the years. Ilfracombe hasn't. Its attraction for visitors has remained, and the welcome and hospitality extended to them is unsurpassed anywhere. Ships' officers and crews as well as passengers liked Ilfracombe. Stepping ashore into the holiday atmosphere was refreshing, even when it was raining. Many life-long friendships developed between Ilfracombe locals and passengers from Swansea, Cardiff, Newport and Bristol. The Devonian Society in Swansea was a good example.

Campbells' first real incursion into the Swansea to Ilfracombe trade started in 1922 with the building of *Glen Gower*. Various ships of the fleet have been based at Swansea since then, some more popular than others. The name *Glen Gower* was just right for Swansea, and the fact that she was a good sea-boat aided her popularity. The history of the port of Ilfracombe merits a book to itself. It was the centre of all down-Channel steamer operations and on occasions saw two or more steamers tied up alongside each other at the pier.

The Birmingham family represented all Campbells' interests in Ilfracombe for many years. Fred, the last of the line of agents there, recently died aged 83. He was a pleasant unflappable character, and as much a part of Ilfracombe as the Pier itself. Campbell's office at No.10 the Quay was owned by the Birmingham family. This is now a shop. For me, passing it brings back many memories of debating in there whether or not to go on some trip or other because of the weather, as hundreds of prospective passengers wended their way down to the Pier, not realising their trip might be off.

Fred Birmingham and Captain Jack George were great friends. On *Bristol Queen* when we had a couple of hours alongside before sailing back up-Channel, and not calling at Lynmouth, Jack would say, 'Mate, I'm going ashore with Fred.' He would change his uniform hat and jacket, and wend his way up the harbour to the Britannia pub. They would be joined there by Bill Irwin and Jack Gant, two of Ilfracombe's great characters, who always kept a weather eye open for the ship's arrival. Bill was a harbour boatman and Jack owned the Lyn Bay Hotel up from the Pier. Although Jack had cooking commitments in his restaurant at that time of the day, he had developed a system which eliminated any possibility of Mrs. Gant knowing he wasn't in the kitchen all the time. Jack Gant had served with Captain George on *Empress Queen* during the War. A couple of halves of Britannia's Best Bitter brought all their log books up to date. At the end of a busy season it was always a pleasure to stay at the Lyn Bay with the Gants. At five guineas a week full board and baby-sitting if required, how could we go wrong?

The Pier from Rapparee Meadows, Ilfracombe.

1895 Ilfracombe. *Bonnie Doon — Lorna Doon — Scotia — Westward Ho — Cambria* and *Brighton*. Lying off is *Alexandria*.

(*Photo by courtesy of Ilfracombe Museum*)

The new Ilfracombe Pier was opened on 31st May, 1952. The old wooden structure was replaced with reinforced concrete. There were two landing faces, the Stone Bench for use at high water times, and the Face of the Pier at others. The 350 ft long South Quay was used on occasions but this was not encouraged. Ships could be berthed alongside one another at both the Face and the Stone Bench, weather and circumstances permitting. Campbells' unique Dolly Fenders were used at all times between ships moored in this manner. The old photograph opposite shows six paddle steamers tied alongside one another at Ilfracombe Pier. It is difficult to believe that this could have happened on any but very few occasions, and that it didn't lead to some sailing sequence difficulty.

The River Avon

Speed limits in the narrow, twisting and violently tidal River Avon between Avonmouth and Bristol were rather restrictive for paddle steamers because of their limited manoeuvrability compared to screw-ships. The transverse thrust of propellers enables a ship to 'tread water' for a period of time. When a paddle-steamer's engines are stopped, control of the ship is lost. It's a great disadvantage, especially when running with the tide. In the 1950s and 1960s there was a lot of shipping up and down the Avon for the Port of Bristol. Instructions on other ships' positions and movements in the river were shouted to you from signal stations passing Avonmouth and at Seamills. There was no VHF contact at that time.

The straight reach of the River between Avonmouth and Pill was the last opportunity to make up some time on the way back up to Bristol. We occasionally took advantage of the river width there, and 'gave her the gun', easing up before getting abeam of Pill. Going up on one of these occasions with *Cardiff Queen* on the top of a large spring tide, the mate said, 'There's a boat with no lights close on the starboard bow.' I reduced speed, but *Cardiff Queen*'s wash carried on regardless. At this point, the river bank on the starboard side is shallow and, on big spring tides such as this one, the river almost invades agricultural land. We berthed at Bristol pontoon, disembarked the passengers, then docked in Cumberland Basin for the night. In the morning, we left there, took the

passengers on board and proceeded down river well before high water. Between Pill and Avonmouth, someone shouted up to the bridge, 'Captain, there's a man in a boat in the middle of that field on the port side, waving to you.' Gesticulating and waving don't always convey the same message. He certainly wasn't waving, having just spent a night in a Somerset field, and hoping that on this next tide there would be sufficient water to float his boat back into the river.

The least we expected was a note from the Haven Master, who controlled all ship operations on the river, and the issue of pilot licences, that *Cardiff Queen* had exceeded the speed limit, and washed a boat into a field. In the spirit of those halcyon days, we heard nothing about it.

When August Bank Holiday was in its rightful place in the calendar, at the beginning of the month, it was usually the best day of the summer season for passengers. 1949 was a good year for weather and business, but Bank Holiday Monday was an exception, with continuous drizzle and poor visibility, and a long run down from Bristol to Ilfracombe and then on to Lundy where we landed a good number of slightly dispirited passengers. It was oilskin and galoshes weather, and by the time we entered the river on the way back to Bristol, Captain George, myself, and many of the Bristol passengers were looking forward to arrival at the pontoon, and into Cumberland Basin for the night.

Unfortunately it was a very small and late neap tide, and to advertise a reasonable arrival time at Bristol, we were scheduled into the river on the very first of the water. The River Avon was often accused of either having too much water or not enough. This time it wasn't enough. On Campbells' ships entering and leaving port and navigating rivers the mate always steered the ship, and the master worked the telegraphs. This wasn't standard practice in every similar company, but with the complexity of Bristol Channel operations it was beneficial in many ways, not least in the experience gained by the mate of taking the ship alongside piers, pontoons and berths. It certainly was the best preparation for a mate's promotion to master, and benefited the degree of co-operation between them on the bridge.

When Jack George said, 'Is she hard a'port, Mate?', and she was, he gave her a bit more engine. The ship still went to starboard, and ended up with the bow stuck in the mud at the entrance to Miles Dock.

Luckily, it was no longer a dock, but a fissure in the Somerset side of the river, so the stern remained afloat. Captain George kept working the engines astern, but *Bristol Queen* wouldn't shift. He then said 'Mate, get the Port After lifeboat down, and run a rope across to the other bank of the river. There's a bollard over there.' The boat was lowered into the water, but we couldn't get it away from the ship's side. The tide was strengthening, and pinning it alongside. *Bristol Queen* suddenly started to move astern, and it was all hands to the lifeboat falls to heave the boat up manually clear of the water. 'All hands' included many of the onlooking passengers, who by then had warmed to the challenge, and were enjoying themselves. The rest of us weren't.

The ship berthed very late at Bristol Pontoon. While the passengers were disembarking, a young man who was standing abreast of the ship's bridge, shouted up to Captain George, 'I understand you've been in trouble.' 'Who are *you*?' said Jack. 'I'm from the newspapers', he replied. 'Well, just you push off now, son, there's nothing for you here.' 'Thank you, sir,' he said, very respectfully, and off he went. What would have happened now, if the media had got their teeth into an incident such as that? Would it have been exaggerated to such a degree as to influence people against travelling on the ships? It happened early on the tide, and the ship was in a fairly safe, but perhaps embarrassing position, with everyone arriving home a couple of hours later than expected. Under similar circumstances and conditions, this wouldn't have happened to *Britannia,* and probably not to *Ravenswood* or *Glen Usk.*

All Ashore that's going Ashore

Considering the conditions in which White Funnel Steamers operated for nearly a century in the Bristol Channel, the number of ships going ashore was relatively few. *Cambria* on Rillage Point at Ilfracombe in 1926, was one. Although there was little damage to the ship, going up on the 'hard' in the Bristol Channel, was very different from taking the ground on one of the many sandbanks.

Captain Bill Watson on *Glen Avon* in 1934, when the ship ended up ashore near Rhoose Point, Barry, was lucky. There was minimal damage, the details of which weren't divulged, although the ship drydocked in Cardiff for an inspection of the bottom. *Glen Avon* was returning from an evening trip to Minehead when she ran ashore in fog on the pebble beach between Rhoose Point and Porthkerry. The ship was ashore for two hours, and to quote the *South Wales Argus* account of the incident, the passengers 'remained cheerful throughout the ordeal, and passed the time in singing and dancing. The postmistress at Rhoose was aroused from her sleep about eleven pm, and it was she who first communicated with the police.' Perhaps it was the singing and dancing which wakened the postmistress, although with only ninety passengers on board *Glen Avon*, it doesn't seem likely.

Coming down-Channel sailing direct to Ilfracombe in 1949 on *Bristol Queen* I said to Captain George, '*Cardiff Queen* seems to be heading at a strange angle for Lynmouth.' ''Yes, Mate,' he said. 'She's ashore on the Sandridge; he's got too much to the West before hauling in. As I've already told you, don't let them at Lynmouth see the ship on the ebb tide until she comes round the Foreland Point.' I never forgot that; perhaps Archie Harris and his mate on *Cardiff Queen* did not on this occasion.

CHANNEL CHARACTERS

WILLIE JAMES was Campbells' traffic manager, the most important job in the Company. The scheduling of many ships in the Bristol and English Channels was his lifetime work. Interchanging, connecting, and ensuring the times he set for vessels to get in and out of piers pontoons and other berths happened, was no easy task. Lifting off the mud at Cardiff, Swansea and Newport and getting ready to take passengers on board and sail to complex schedules advertised months in advance was only done with confidence born of long experience. When Willie James died, things which had been taken for granted became problems. It is said that you can't take it with you. Well, Willie did, and the hunt for a successor was on. **Alec Taylor**, his assistant and son of **Captain Dan Taylor**, former commodore master of the Company, didn't want the job. Alec had been brought up in Campbells like his brother **Johnny Taylor**, chief engineer of *Glen Usk*. **Jack Guy,** another lifetime member of the White Funnel shore staff in Cardiff, fell heir to the title. With so many old hands still in charge of the ships, that aspect of the operations went along much the same. Scheduling fourteen ships before the War was very different from half that number afterwards.

JACK GUY was a member of a family of Cardiff tug owners. They had been associated with Campbells for many years. Jack was very much a part of the Cardiff Pierhead scene. He knew everyone in and around Tiger Bay, the famous and the infamous, and they all knew him. Jack's long experience in handling countless thousands of passengers stood him in good stead. He knew when things were going right, and the right places to go when they weren't. The two pontoons at Cardiff pierhead provided four berths for the ships: the South, the North, the Bristol and the Burnham berths. All that remains now, with the building of the Cardiff Barrage, are the wooden dolphins sticking out of the water. Perhaps they can be retained as a permanent memorial to a hundred years at the centre of Bristol Channel passenger activities.

REG KENNEY was chief steward of *Ravenswood* in 1948, and had been a steward with Campbells before the War. He was very particular about everything served from 'his' pantry to the dining saloon. He was also fastidious about his own appearance, and the appearance of the restaurants and bars in his care. Before he started work as a boy, his father said to him 'Reg, whatever jobs you take, make sure you are handling money. You'll get to know the value of it, and most importantly you'll never be short.' When the War started, he was interviewed for a job in the aircraft works at Filton, Bristol. When asked what he did, he replied 'a Chief on the ships.' This could have been misinterpreted as Chief Engineer. He got the job, learned to read a micrometer, became a 'progress chaser', and was set up with a home job in a reserved occupation for the rest of the War.

Captain C.H. McANALLY was shore agent in Swansea in the 1950s. Mac was a retired master from B.P. Tankers. Throughout the summer he lived in Campbells' office on Pockett's Wharf, going home to Ffairfach, Llandeilo at the end of the season. Used as he was to the big ships, Mac found it difficult to understand some of our antics with paddlers. He was always meticulous, helpful, and a good friend.

BOB CAMPBELL was the elder son of the founder of the Company. To us newcomers in 1948, Bob appeared to be, and acted as, a member of a remote generation. As Weston Agent for the ships, we had a lot to do—or not to do—with him, and as 'youngsters' in the business, the less the better. Bob was always right, even when he was wrong. Eventually he left the country and retired to Ireland.

JOHN HALE was the Newport agent, and a retired policeman. In those days Newport had its own boat, usually *Ravenswood* or *Glen Usk*, although *Glen Gower* and even *Cardiff Queen* did stints there when

Presentation of plaque in recognition of service to the Boys' Brigade at Newport. 1953

homeward passage. The radio licence didn't appear to cover the TV receiver. I asked the postmaster at Wind Street Post Office to issue a licence to the ship. He said it was a precedent, and would be the first time this had happened. The first TV licence to be issued to a ship was in the name of *Cardiff Queen*. The TV proved a great attraction for quite some time, until a lady came into the dining saloon and said, 'I came here to get away from that.' We took it off the ship shortly afterwards.

HARRY LIBBY. The re-opening of Mumbles Pier coincided with Harry's year of office as mayor of Swansea. It was necessary for Campbells to appoint a Mumbles booking agent. Libby's agency in the Dunns was the obvious choice. Mr.Smith-Cox hadn't met Harry previous to our visit. After the arrangements were made, he produced photos of ships at the old pier going back to the turn of the century. Passengers coming ashore and looking up at the cameraman was a popular snap. Smith-Cox thumbed through them with interest. 'Mr Libby,' he said, looking at the long black dresses and the large flowerpot hats which dominated the pictures, 'I now understand why the divorce rate was so low in those days. The women all looked the same.'

required. Sticking the ship's bow into the mud to swing on the flood tide was a unique operation. It was particularly unique at night, near high water, when the two or three yards of grass at the top of the river bank were occupied by courting couples unaware (until it was too late) that a ship's bow would be ploughing into the grass to keep them company. The screams heard were, at least sometimes, for the wrong reasons.

LES BANBURY was the pioneer of TV in Swansea. He demonstrated and sold the first television sets in the area, and was a good supporter of the ships. In 1954, Les put the latest model on board *Cardiff Queen* for a trial. On an off-service day the crew rigged a dipole aerial at the top of the mainmast, connected up to a seventeen-inch Ferguson set in the dining saloon. Few homes had sets then. It was a great attraction, particularly on the last trip at night from Ilfracombe. The children would sit around watching, giving the parents a bit of leeway during the

Television licence for *Cardiff Queen*: it was the first time for one to be issued to a ship.

69

Harry had many stories to tell. Churchill's visit after the Blitz was one of them. Councillors were lined up at the Guildhall to meet the great man. First in line was Harry Libby. 'My name's Churchill, what's yours?' Winston said. Harry really liked that.

Captain CLIVE SPENCER started his sea-going life as an Ordinary Seaman on *Ravenswood* in 1952, aged fourteen. I now understand he said he was sixteen to get the job. From *Ravenswood* Clive went to sea properly, got his time in, and got his first command in 1974. In 1979 he became a ships' pilot there, and is now the senior harbour pilot in a north Australian Port, and looking forward to retirement in a couple of years time from a very successful career in shipping; it all began with a season on *Ravenswood*. In 1989 Clive wrote an article on his experiences there in 1952, and followed that up with a number of interesting letters. I think he does rate as a

Captain Clive Spencer, former Ordinary Seaman, *Ravenswood.*

Channel Character. He used to help when he was twelve years old, taking our ropes on Penarth Pier, assisting another character of the day, Piermaster Stan Galley.

BETTY GUNN. My wife's claim to the status of Channel Character is the length of her sea-going career. By August 1958 it was clear that weather conditions and business didn't justify dining saloon waiters on *Cardiff Queen* with daily sailings across Channel from Swansea. It was agreed in discussion with Smith-Cox and Vic Taylor the chief steward, that they should be paid off and revert to a buffet-type service in the dining saloon. Who was going to run the buffet? Mr. Smith-Cox and Vic Taylor suggested my wife. It was only for a few weeks and the season would be over. Four passages between Swansea and Ilfracombe was the usual Saturday sailing schedule. Because of the weather, I was on the bridge continually for the first three passages,

Outside the new Booking Office at Ferryport. Betty and the rest of the staff. Betty booked the tickets, ordered stores, paid repair bills, Dai was watchman, car park attendant, ropeman, helped with water, stores and bunkering. He made sure everyone got on board safely during the night and made doubly sure they got up in time in the morning.

until the ship arrived in Ilfracombe the second time. I went down below to see how my wife and the buffet were getting on. The steward said, 'She got off at Mumbles Pier on the way out this time.' A short sea-going career, maybe, but the weather really *was* bad!

SHIPBOARD ENTERTAINMENT

Traditionally, P.& A. Campbell didn't have entertainment on board their ships. They depended on efficiency, punctuality, and most important, sunshine and good weather to attract passengers. Charterers, as is usual, made arrangements with the company for any music or entertainment they wished to put on board the ship. Exclusive chartered ships were less frequent than one might expect. This may have been one of the weaknesses of the company's post-War activities. Sales and marketing were never a strong point. There was little leeway in the pre-season scheduling of the ships to allow for unforeseen lucrative charters, and prospective charterers had to do the chasing.

Clifton Smith-Cox wasn't a person who waited for the sun to shine, hoping passengers would come along. He set out to find them. His changes didn't always get the thumbs-up from traditionalists. Some of them worked out, others didn't. It is still difficult to say whether regular entertainment on board ships then boosted passenger numbers. Showboats, jazz cruises, solo singers, stand-up comics, sit-down seasick comics: we had them all. Too young at that time to be a traditionalist, I enjoyed it, and got to know many interesting people I wouldn't have met otherwise. Unfortunately the steamers weren't the best venues for many types of performance. The only real area for this is the top deck, and to give of their best, artists often found that 18 knots into a fresh westerly wasn't exactly what they had signed on for. Many of the artists engaged for these trips had been very well-known entertainers in their day. Others were starting in the business, making their way up the ladder, via the gangway. Going back on board one evening I stopped a couple of musicians coming off *Glen Usk* at Cardiff. 'What's the name of your band?' I asked one of them. 'Acker Bilk', he said. 'Acker Bilk?' I repeated. 'Son, you'll never get anywhere with a name like that.' How wrong can one get? My very belated apology—forty years on—to Mr. Bilk.

On a *Cardiff Queen* showboat trip from Bristol. June Powell was singing to an audience of two: me and the helmsman.

WINTERING WITH CAMPBELLS

We were often asked by passengers, 'What do you do in the winter?' The answer was, 'Have a holiday, look after the ships, and get ready for next season.'

P. & A. had long experience in seasonal employment, and understood the need to keep qualified personnel. The operation of paddle steamers, especially on the bridge and in the engine-room, was a specialised job. Employing officers without offering year-round work would have been disastrous. Not everyone wanted it, but if you lived in or near Bristol it was a must. The low weekly wage was no incentive. The attraction for most of us who had spent our lives until then sailing round the world on long voyages was being able to live at home for several months of the year. This easily compensated for the long hours in the summer.

It may come as a surprise to learn that in 1949-1950 the weekly remuneration for a mate with a first mate or master's certificate was £6.50 to £7.00, while a steward's boy before the War earned £5.00 a week plus tips, with no qualifications. That didn't seem to balance. The difference was, of course, that senior officers were paid all year round; chocolate boys and others weren't, only when they were working.

P. & A. Campbell were not members of the Shipping Federation, but had a seasonal connection with the Seaman's Union. Officers' rates of salary were in many cases individually agreed, based on past performance and current importance to the company. This didn't affect newcomers like me, but I am sure that the Branders, the Georges, and other long time servants may have wondered about each other. My quick progress up the ladder, to £9 as first mate of *Empress Queen*, and a few weeks later £13 as master of *Glen Gower* was really something. In 1949, a pint of George's Best Bitter was ten pence.

The maintenance, care and attention the ships received over the winter was quite exceptional. Almost everything was 'in house' at the Underfall Yard in Bristol. Any work required on board could be carried out by Company employees—shipwrights, carpentry, plumbing, electrical, and of course all painting except the underwater section of the hull when in drydock, for the annual renewal of the passenger certificates. Before the War when the ships drydocked in Charles Hill's Bristol Yard, Campbell men went over the side and did all the hull painting. This practice was discontinued when compulsory safety rules were introduced into the shipyard.

The Underfall Yard foundry cast all the metal bushes for the steamers' paddle-wheels. They were seldom renewed. After the Yard closed and the ships moved from Bristol to Penarth, bushes became a persistent problem. The wear on them became an increasing reason for delays and unusual expense. The Campbell formula was not passed on, and was never duplicated .

Harry Granville was in charge of painting the vessels. Nothing was too good for them, and nobody could paint a ship inside and out to the Granville standard. The design and workmanship on Campbell's paddle steamers couldn't be bettered.

The master of each ship looked after the lifesaving and firefighting equipment. The mate and bosun and a crew member, if available, scrubbed and varnished decks, de-scaled inside the hull and paddle boxes and generally prepared the ship for winter lay-up, making an early start on preparations for sailing in the spring. The dining saloon, bars, restaurants, galleys and pantries were cleaned and painted by a gang made up of stewards and pursers as available. Everyone mucked in, and every ship came out of lay-up in as near-perfect condition as was possible.

A Motoring Interlude

Car parking at the winter lay-up berths of the ships never presented any great problem for the officers and crews because in the early 1950s cars were few and far between. Alex Campbell had a Standard 8 Saloon; Roger Whyte, second engineer of *Ravenswood*, had a Wolseley. Leo

Ravenswood and *Westward Ho* at Howells Dock before the War, preparing for the season.

Virgo and Gwyn Edwards were motorcyclists, Gwyn with the added comfort of a sidecar. The fact that Leo and Gwyn had both defected about the same time from Bristol Steam Navigation Company to Campbells was coincidental to their choice of transport. The 84 bus from Bristol City Centre was the main form of transport for the rest of us not living in the immediate vicinity of the ships.

A lift in Alex Campbell's Standard was frequently on offer and generally accepted. With Alex at the wheel, Captain Bert Murphy in the back seat and at least two more small ones crammed in, the Standard was often down to its marks. There was no other way of loading the car. When both Bert and Alex were in the front, either the passenger door wouldn't close or Alex couldn't turn the wheel. The vehicle was well down by the stern under these conditions, severely restricting its performance. The only times we passed a bus on Hotwells Road was at a bus stop. Bert usually got out fairly early in the ride. This had a major de-ballasting effect, or the climb from the Centre up the Gloucester Road to Bishopston could have presented difficulties.

Roger Whyte our second engineer gave me my very first driving lessons in his Wolseley. We normally went out at lunch time. It appeared to interest Captain Brander. He lived on board *Glen Usk* all summer and winter, only going home to Scotland at Christmas and New Year. After I'd returned one day from a lesson, Brander said, 'Captain, can I have a wee word with you? I see you're driving that car. I thought I'd just mention that sailors don't make very good drivers, you know. They are used to keeping to the starboard side, and driving on the left in a motorcar can be confusing and dangerous.' I thought at the time he was joking but on reflection realised because his only interests were the ships, the company and those working for it, that the advice was given with the best of intentions.

Leslie H. Brooks, mate of *Ravenswood* then of *Cardiff Queen* had been in the car ownership category for many years before the War. Having started off with a Ford, he never changed his allegiance, and still ran Fords throughout his service with Campbells. Perhaps his initial experiences as an owner are worth a mention here. Les was from Lancashire and lived in Newport. He had started his sea-career as a deck-apprentice with Evan Thomas Radcliffe of Cardiff, well-known

owners of a fleet of foreign-going trampships. Prior to joining Campbells he had been master of an F.T. Everard coastal tanker. He was the unofficial Captain of Malapropism, and in his own words 'would frequently revile us with his antidotes'.

Les's family were Lancashire mill owners, and when his inheritance came through he bought his first car in Liverpool from a 'reputable' dealer who showed him how to drive it so he could take it away with him. His account of how he and Mrs. Brooks took the car from Liverpool back home to Newport after his 30 minutes' driving lesson is quite unique, or at least I hope it was.

As was the norm in those days, the car had three forward gears and reverse with no syncromesh, requiring double de-clutching to change gear. On the first steep hill the car stopped halfway up; the dealer hadn't told him anything about changing down. When he started her up again, the car kept running back as the half-hour tuition hadn't included hill starts. This was being watched with interest by a gang of workmen at

Cardiff Queen at Combe. Les 'reviling' passengers with some of his 'antidotes'. Mother seems to be more interested in the cameraman.

the roadside who offered to help by placing a brick behind one of the rear wheels, so that Les could then put the car in first gear and drive up the hill changing up as necessary until the next enforced stop.

Although the car was at the top of the first hill, what about the others ahead? They realised then they weren't out of the wood yet, so Mrs. Brooks went back down, retrieved the brick and took it into the car. That is how they got back home to Newport with their first car. It was never disclosed how many more hills they encountered on the way, or how long the trip took, but I understand that the brick became a family heirloom.

By the time Les became chief officer of *Cardiff Queen* he had obtained his Advanced Drivers' licence which had pride of place on the windscreen of his 'Ford Perfect'.

Riding pillion on a motorcycle was another new Campbells experience. Our purser on *Ravenswood*, Jim Keating, invited Virgo and me to visit his home in the Forest of Dean. Leo picked me up at the Golden Lion on Gloucester Road. 'Just put your arms around me and hold tight. We won't be stopping on the way, and I don't swerve for animals.' I was rather concerned about the animals bit. Cats and dogs OK, but what about sheep and cows? My driver was well-protected against the winter weather, and when we arrived at Jim's the warmth of the Irish hospitality soon thawed me out. Apprehension about the return trip in the dark was temporarily dispelled.

Every P.& A. ship I sailed on was well-manned, but the combination of Virgo as mate, Alex Campbell as chief engineer and Jim Keating as purser, could hardly be bettered. It made for a happily-efficient ship. Despite *Ravenswood*'s shortcomings, not enough steam when you needed it, limited comforts and amenities for crew and passengers, and other similar slight inconveniences, she was a very popular ship (Briton Ferry excepted). Older passengers liked *Ravenswood*'s friendly charm. She wasn't expected to do much, and usually succeeded.

Another form of complementary transport was Gwyn Edwards' sidecar. Living beside him in Downend, I had the pleasure of some exciting trips between Downend and Chipping Sodbury, where we usually went for evening refreshments. In these days we seldom encountered other vehicles on passage.

I bought my first car from Neville Cottman. It was a 1931 Morris Minor. Prior to joining Campbells, Neville worked in the Bristol Shipping Federation. He received the car as a present from a grateful mother whose son he had managed to get away to sea. Neville couldn't drive, the lady wanted rid of the car, so he let me have it for £16. From what we knew, apart from Neville, this car had one careful owner who kept it on blocks in the garage where we picked it up for transfer to Downend. Jack Lamb's garage there put it in full working order for £6.15s.11d. Total cost on the road £22.15s.11d. My *ex-gratia* payment for towing *Bristol Queen* to safety on 19th August 1956 subsidised it. Petrol shortages during the Suez Crisis restricted driving tests, but I took the liberty of giving myself a dispensation. There was little else on the road anyway, and it was nice to be independently mobile for the first time.

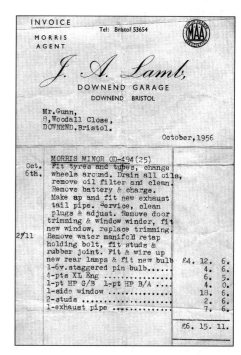

THE BRISTOL CHANNEL HOVERCRAFT

P.S. CARDIFF QUEEN AND WESTLAND HOVERCRAFT S.R.N.2.

In 1963, Clifton Smith-Cox decided that a regular car ferry service across the Bristol Channel between Cardiff and Weston was needed. Previous attempts to establish this had failed because of the very high tidal rise and fall. The cost of providing suitable berthing facilities was quite impractical and the operation, if based on irregular times due to the tides, would be unsatisfactory. He felt that irrespective of the imminent Severn Bridge, it would be a competitive route for motorists. There was sufficient regular vehicular traffic between the catchment areas of Weston to justify a regular service that could only be provided, under the circumstances, by hovercraft.

Negotiations took place between P.& A. Campbell and Westland Aircraft Ltd., with a view to introducing a hovercraft capable of carrying two hundred passengers or twenty cars, or a combination of both. It was therefore decided jointly by Westland and Campbells to operate an experimental service with SRN 2 for six weeks in the summer of 1963. This was a passenger-carrying craft only, and would be run in conjunction with the usual steamer services between Cardiff and Weston. Hovercraft passengers would be able to spend a day in south Wales and return to Weston by steamer and vice-versa. In order to allow the maximum number of people to travel by hovercraft, only single tickets each way would be booked. The introduction of this experimental hovercraft service was in every way to complement the existing steamer services between Cardiff and Weston.

On the basis of the experiment, Townsend Ferries Limited then proceeded to operate hovercraft services from Dover for a couple of years, before deciding to revert to ship only services across the English Channel. Westland Aircraft provided their most experienced test pilots who had been involved with hovercraft development since its inception. They were Captain P.M. Lamb, Captain H. Phillips, and T. Kennedy, engineer.

SRN 2 arriving at Cardiff Docks in 1963.

(Photograph by courtesy of Eric Brown, Derby)

A BRISTOL CHANNEL VEHICLE FERRY: COSTS AND COMPLICATIONS

In 1969, P.& A. Campbell—by then a member of European Ferries Group—agreed a feasibility study for the operation of a passenger and freight service between Swansea and Ilfracombe. The new Ferryport at Swansea was the attraction. Now, almost 30 years later, some local authorities are expressing a similar interest. In 1968 our discussions with British Transport Board in Swansea confirmed their interest in supporting another ferry service from the new berth in conjunction with the B.& I. project to Ireland. Roland Wickenden, Chairman of European ferries, agreed to go ahead with a survey. Overseas consultants experienced in passenger-ferry studies were appointed. They said that only Swansea to Ilfracombe could be viable for this kind of service. The depths of water to be dredged to would guarantee a regular service from Swansea.

Ilfracombe was a different proposition. A berth completely detached from the pier would have to be designed and installed. Initial thoughts were for a floating pontoon with a ramp to the shore on the south side of the Harbour. On 31st July, 1969 I sent this memo to Mr. Smith-Cox:- *At the Council Meeting in Ilfracombe on Tuesday evening, the Council voted unanimously in approval of a proposed vehicle/passenger ferry service between Swansea and Ilfracombe. It was made perfectly clear to them that the project is merely in its initial inquiry stage, and that most of their many questions could only receive hypothetical answers, which I felt were satisfactory for the time being. Should you wish, I shall go into more detail when we meet. GSG.*

We considered using *Autocarrier*—a converted GSN Thames pleasure-steamer becoming redundant on the Dover to Zeebrugge service. The Zeebrugge Pontoon Berth would also be used if suitable. Townsend's marine superintendent sent me a condition report of the Pontoon Berth. I visited Zeebrugge, had a look at it and the ship in operation in the Brugge Canal Lock. It wasn't suitable for Bristol Channel use. The Pontoon was scrapped. *Autocarrier* was sold to the Italians, and ran ashore somewhere in the Mediterranean. The results of the feasibility study were awaited before plans for a car-ferry in the Bristol Channel could go ahead, and it took longer than expected.

We wanted to investigate the practical operation of the ship; operational and capital costs and financial viability; the impact of the Severn Bridge; motorway extensions into the West Country; who would use the service; where 'cut off' points would be for Midlands, Wales and the West. Evaluating foot-passengers, cars, coaches and caravans was fairly easy, but what about freight? When in doubt, try the University. We did, and found that one of their departments had been monitoring vehicles crossing the Severn Bridge since it opened three years previously. Statistics and information from their study of the Bridge were most helpful to the consultants.

It was clear that the size and draft of the ship necessary for this service would be very different from anything that had ever used Ilfracombe before. The investigation into the possibility of suitable berthing and landing facilities at Ilfracombe started by discussion with the Oceanography Department at University College, Swansea. We required a complete under sea-bed and hydrographic survey of the harbour. This was to ascertain if it was possible to dredge to sufficient depths to construct a non-tidal area for continuous ferry operations. The only equipment for the work was owned and operated by Kelvin Hughes. Promises were made for us to have the use of the equipment but it didn't materialise. Because of this the projected survey had to be postponed.

We chartered the University vessel *Ocean Crest* to carry out an initial ground survey. Provisional dates for the main survey were 14/16 April, 22nd April, and 27th May but were all cancelled: equipment was promised, but then not available. It was all very frustrating. In July a survey was attempted with limited results in unsuitable weather conditions. But some results were quite encouraging.

In August the survey equipment was made available again, and some of it was transported from Barry to Ilfracombe by *Balmoral*. The full survey of the harbour was done and the depths to bedrock were estimated. In order to check out our results we waited until September's very large spring tides, hired a digger and at low water excavated in a number of spots where the survey had shown that bedrock existed. Our findings matched the survey exactly. A lot had gone into this survey. It was a great feeling at the time.

The Consultants submitted their very comprehensive report in July 1970. This covered all aspects of the operation of a ferry between Swansea and Ilfracombe. Herewith a short analysis. The Ferry should accommodate 120 cars, 600/700 passengers. It should operate two round trips per day Jan.-April, Oct.-Dec.; with three to four trips per day in summer. The viability of the operation depended on the carriage of passengers, cars and freight. A passenger-only operation was very limited seasonally, and weather-dependent for survival. Ilfracombe could handle foot-passenger traffic, but a complete new terminal facility to cope with vehicular movements would have to be built. Whether it was possible for access to and from the harbour at Ilfracombe to take the size of freight vehicles envisaged in the future would have to be determined.

The main specification for the ferry would be 2,200 gross tons; length overall 250 ft.; beam 50 ft.; max. draft 11 ft.; Main Engines 8,000 h.p.; Aux.450 h.p. x 3; Bow Thrust Unit 600 h.p; Service Speed 17.5 knots; approx. cost of ferry (1970) £1,800,000.

As it turned out, European Ferries decided not to go ahead with this project. One reason given was the rapid development of Dover and Zeebrugge, and the necessity to invest their money in new tonnage for the English-Channel routes.

Now, in 1997 the physical aspects of a cross-channel operation are not very different from what they were in 1970, but the other factors would need to be determined again.

EPILOGUE

The end of the White Funnel paddle-steamer operations came in 1967 when *Bristol Queen* was taken out of service. One year before that *Cardiff Queen* had suffered the same fate.

Campbells' had already acquired a small twin-screw motor ship from the Red Funnel Company of Southampton, and named her *Westward Ho* after one of the fine pre-War paddle steamers which gave great service to the Company in the Bristol Channel. This was augmented by another redundant and smaller ship *St.Trillo* from the Liverpool and North Wales Steamship Co. Neither, or both together, fulfilled the requirements expected from P.& A. Campbell White Funnel ships, even though economics dictated that the only viable operational situation which could exist at that time was small twin-screw diesel tonnage.

A criterion for economy, comparable comfort, efficiency and reliability was later established with the acquisition from Red Funnel of M.V. *Balmoral*, which is still running today under the ownership of Waverley Steam Navigation Co. Ltd. It is fair to say that *Balmoral* has provided the link in the chain of continuity of Bristol Channel sailings for many years, and is as popular with passengers throughout the British Isles as she always had been, as part of the Red Funnel fleet from Southampton, and later with Campbells in the Bristol Channel.

The withdrawal from service in 1980 of *Balmoral* signalled the demise of Campbells in the Bristol Channel. This was a very sad moment for many who had long involvement with the ships and the Company.

There is always some light at the end of a tunnel. It came in the Paddle Steamer Preservation Society's re-incarnation of *Waverley* and *Balmoral*. *Waverley*—now the last sea-going paddle-steamer in the world—has been operating regularly in Spring and Autumn in the Bristol Channel since 1979, and *Balmoral* has been maintaining a full summer service since 1986. Now restored to traditional White Funnel colours, she is a living survivor of the great White Funnel Fleet. I wish to end this book with a tribute to those who have worked so hard to 'keep the wheels turning' when all seemed lost, particularly Terry Sylvester and Captain David Neil.

Information regarding sailings in the Bristol Channel and elsewhere around the UK by *Waverley* and *Balmoral* can be obtained from: Waverley Excursions Ltd., Gwalia Buildings, Barry Docks CF62 5QR, Tel. 01446 720656. Long may they continue!